Library and Library-Related Publications

Library and Library-Related Publications

A Directory of
Publishing Opportunities
in Journals, Serials,
and Annuals

by

Peter Hernon, Maureen Pastine, and

Sara Lou Williams

1973

Libraries Unlimited, Inc.
Littleton, Colo.

LIBRARIES UNLIMITED, INC.
P.O. Box 263
Littleton, Colorado 80120

CONTENTS

INTRODUCTION

PURPOSE OF THE DIRECTORY

Library and Library-Related Publications lists publishing opportunities for librarianship and at the same time describes the general
orientation of each periodical, serial, and annual included. It is addressed to
librarians who would like to contribute articles and who want detailed
information about the various publications. Although the directory serves as a
current, basic compilation for publications in library science and related
areas, this is not its primary purpose. *Ulrich's International Periodicals
Directory* and *The Directory of Library Periodicals*[1] are much more complete
in this respect. *Ulrich's* includes periodicals on an international basis;
newsletters; state, county and local publications; periodicals not indexed; and
publications of specialized library associations such as law and medicine. *The
Directory of Library Periodicals* lacks descriptive information but contains
approximately 800 entries for American periodicals including newsletters and
minor or local publications with limited distribution. Naturally, this 1967
work is dated; there have been changes in editorship and titles, and some
periodicals have been discontinued. One additional source deserves mention:
Winckler's *Library Periodicals*[2] provides a list of approximately 160
periodicals, American and foreign, with scattered annotations. Like *The
Directory of Library Periodicals*, it does not suggest publishing opportunities.
Our directory is selective in that it primarily lists journals, serials,
and annuals published in the United States and, with some notable
exceptions, excludes the assorted material contained in *Ulrich's* or *The
Directory of Library Periodicals*. It is hoped that the entries in this directory
provide much more extensive information about each source than the other
listings of publications for librarianship. Such information is essential because
titles of publications can be misleading, with the result that a manuscript
might be sent to an inappropriate source. For example, the Graduate Library
School *Bulletin* for the University of Chicago does not publish manuscripts.
Instead, it reviews children's books; reviews are written by the editor and
submitted to a committee. Naturally such a bulletin does not fit into the
scope of this directory; therefore, it is not included. The *ASLIB Occasional
Publications* and *Reference Services Review*, a reviewing source published by
Pierian Press, are other examples. Since the ASLIB publications are the
research reports of the ASLIB Research Department, they do not accept
unsolicited manuscripts. This directory, however, does include certain serial
and annual publications of interest to potential authors who have manuscripts
too long for inclusion in typical journals. Primarily these sources are
monographic series, occasional paper series, and annuals such as "Advances in
Librarianship."

To increase the value of this directory, there is a subject index by which authors can easily determine publications for which their manuscript will be best suited. It is always helpful to know several alternative sources to which a particular manuscript can be sent in case one publisher rejects it. Appendix I contains an additional selective list of monographic series for which complete information was not available.

Library science, like other subject areas, is marked by the proliferation of published material. Glancing at *Ulrich's* and *Library Literature* confirms the fact that there are many periodicals relating directly or indirectly to several aspects of librarianship. Indeed, this confirms the interdisciplinary nature of the field. Many periodicals serve a specific purpose and meet specific needs.

The increase in the number of periodicals and serials has had a tremendous impact upon the library profession, making it difficult for authors and potential authors to keep abreast of all the latest trends either in the general field or in an area of special interest. Authors are not always aware of the general orientation of these publications, or of the opportunities they might provide for publishing.

Authors seeking publication of a manuscript can encounter difficulties in locating a publisher. Of course, most librarians are familiar with publications such as *Library Journal, Library Trends, College and Research Libraries, Special Libraries, RQ,* and *Occasional Papers* published by the Graduate School of Library Science at the University of Illinois. But what about journals that are not as well known—those that are only indirectly related to the library field, or other occasional papers and irregular series? Moreover, even with respect to the publications just mentioned, contributors often do not realize the exact specifications required; these vary from periodical to periodical. What style, if any, is recommended? Is an inquiry or an abstract necessary? How long does evaluation take? What type of article does the publisher want? How many copies of a manuscript should be submitted? Glancing through the periodical or looking on the inside cover will not always answer these questions adequately. In effect, submission of a manuscript is, in part, a guessing game. One must often assume that it will be of interest to that particular publication and that the correct or recommended procedure is being followed.

Heretofore, librarians have had to rely upon the few sources available or upon the publications themselves, in order to obtain information about the publishing opportunities and/or general requirements for library-related publications. *Writers' Market* (1971) devotes less than two pages to library science and covers only five periodicals. As a result, this source is so weak for the field of librarianship that it can be bypassed. The *Directory of Scholarly and Research Publishing Opportunities* (1971)[3] is divided into five major sections: general; humanities; social sciences; science and technology; and sports, games, and hobbies. The section on library science is quite brief and is highly selective. It even excludes some of the better-known periodicals such as *Drexel Library Quarterly*, *Library Journal*, *Special Libraries*, and *Library Trends*. Although *Magazines for Libraries*, by Bill Katz,[4] includes a section on library periodicals, its entries are primarily brief descriptions of general or popular periodicals in the field and do not include all the information needed by manuscript contributors.

As this directory was being compiled, an attempt was made to cover all available sources, including such well-known indexes as *Library Literature*, *Ulrich's*, *Irregular Serials and Annuals*, etc. State publications are included on a selective basis. Each state issues such publications but it is not uncommon for them to be limited to contributors within the state. Outside contributions are sometimes accepted if they are relevant or of interest to librarians within the state. There is usually no payment for publication.

Our correspondence with the editorial staffs of the various publications revealed that a few publications do not solicit manuscripts from outside contributors. For example, libraries might issue bulletins or papers that are compilations of staff articles or articles written by users of their collections. These publications have been included on a selective basis. The same selectivity applies to proceedings and conference papers, lectures, and occasional papers. Proceedings are often a collection of papers and meetings held at annual conferences and later published as part of a series. They include only works of participants at the particular conference. Publications that consist of a collection of lectures delivered at a particular institution are generally deleted, since they are of limited value to potential authors seeking a source of publication. In addition, occasional monographic series that cover primarily non-library related subjects do not fit into the scope of this directory.

Automation, datamation, and computer journals that accept library-related articles are listed. Educational periodicals are included, particularly if they accept for publication manuscripts related to library education. Additional sources for education may be found in the *Directory of Scholarly and Research Publishing Opportunities* (pp. 186-207) and in William Camp's *Guide to Periodicals in Education* (1968).[5] Camp incorporates publishing information for 449 nationally distributed education periodicals; thus, although it is older than the *Directory of Scholarly and Research Publishing Opportunities*, it is more comprehensive.

Most of the information in this directory was gathered from questionnaires sent to the editors of periodicals. Basically, only those publications that responded to the questionnaire are included. In certain instances, it was requested that a particular publication not be included in the directory. The data gathered have been compiled under the following headings for each entry:

Title and subtitle (if any)
Address of publication
Subscription price
Circulation

9

Frequency of issue
Editor (if known)
Address of editor (included only if different from the address of the
        publication)
Indexed or abstracted in
Description of the publication
Contributors
Style requirements
Number of manuscript copies to submit
Approximate length of manuscript
Abstract requirement (i.e., whether the author should submit a short
        synopsis of the article before sending the manuscript for
        evaluation)
Evaluation time
Payment
Additional information

Publications change editorship, have policy revisions, cease publication, or come into existence. As a result, directories listing journals, series, and annuals quickly become dated, if not obsolete. *Library and Library-Related Publications* can be periodically updated and expanded, and any suggestions as to possible future inclusions would be appreciated by the authors.

Because so many persons, knowingly or not, helped to make this directory possible, we can specifically acknowledge only our major indebtedness. Our profound gratitude is expressed to the editors and editorial staff members of the publications responding to the questionnaire. Elena Hill provided invaluable assistance in her initial searching through various library and library-related periodicals.

SENDING THE MANUSCRIPT

A manuscript submitted for evaluation should be accompanied by a letter briefly explaining its value and timeliness and requesting appraisal of the work in case it is not accepted. The letter should also request acknowledgement of the manuscript's receipt. In order to ensure prompt consideration of the manuscript, the author may ask the editor to evaluate the article within a set time period. If the editor is unable to meet this deadline, he will generally inform the author that evaluation will take longer. In the event that the editor does not write, the author may send a letter of inquiry after a reasonable length of time. It occasionally happens that the editorial staff forgets about a manuscript; an inquiry from the author could regenerate interest.

Most library or library-related periodicals promptly acknowledge receipt of manuscripts. If a manuscript is not accepted for publication, usually it will be returned in the self-addressed stamped envelope submitted with the manuscript. Policies vary as to whether rejected manuscripts are criticized. At times an editor might suggest a periodical for which the topic might be more suitable.

Obviously, all manuscripts should be typed double-spaced with wide margins. This increases the likelihood that returned manuscripts will contain editorial comments. Some editors comment only if there is appropriate room on the manuscript. In addition, some periodicals require a short synopsis of the article upon either submission or publication of the manuscript; information about abstract requirements is included for each entry in the directory. Except for a few instances, which are mentioned in the directory, editors prefer that the author's name, position, and affiliation be on a separate page, so that manuscripts can be sent anonymously to the editorial staff.

Although many library-related publications make no payment for manuscripts they publish, they provide authors with from two to fifty free copies of the issue or article. In a few cases (noted in the directory), journals do not pay for individual articles but offer an honorarium for the best article of the year as judged by the editorial staff.

At present, library and library-related publications are bombarded with materials, and some of them are encountering budgetary restrictions. *American Libraries*, for example, fits into this category and will not accept feature material for publication in 1973. Both *College and Research Libraries* and *Special Libraries* have tremendous backlogs of manuscripts awaiting publication and might not accept all timely articles. Many of the occasional paper series, monographic series, and other irregular or infrequent publications are also experiencing budgetary limitations, and some have ceased publication for an indefinite period of time. It is because of these difficulties that potential authors need the type of information provided in this directory.

FOOTNOTES

1. Mary A. Springman and Betty M. Brown, *The Directory of Library Periodicals*, Drexel Library School Series, No. 23 (Philadelphia: Drexel Press, 1967).

2. Paul A. Winckler, *Library Periodicals: A Selected List of Periodicals Relating to Library Work* (Brookville, N.Y.: C. W. Post College, 1963). There is also a 1967 edition which is somewhat enlarged; nevertheless, many of the periodicals listed in Winckler have ceased publication.

3. Alvin Renetzky, *Directory of Scholarly and Research Publishing Opportunities* (Orange, N.J.: Academic Media, 1971).

4. Bill Katz and Berry Gargal, *Magazines for Libraries: For the General Reader and School, Junior College, College and Public Libraries*, 2nd ed. (New York: R. R. Bowker Co., 1972), pp. 474-96.

5. William L. Camp, *Guide to Periodicals in Education* (Metuchen, N.J.: Scarecrow Press, Inc., 1968).

LIBRARY PERIODICALS

AB BOOKMAN'S WEEKLY: The Specialist Book Trade Weekly
(formerly *Antiquarian Bookman*)

AB Bookman's Weekly and Bookman's Yearbook
Antiquarian Bookman for the Specialist Book World
Box 1100
Newark, New Jersey 07101

Subscription: $14.50; single issue, $0.75
Circulation: 5,500
Frequency: Weekly

Editor: Sol M. Malkin

Indexed in: Library Literature

Description: Discussions and speeches within the book trade, quotes from
               several annual library reports, and reprints of pertinent
               articles that have not received more than local circulation.

Contributors: Contributors are not limited primarily to librarians, and
               there is no policy of accepting more than one manuscript
               per year from a contributor.

Style requirements: Not specified

Number of manuscript
copies to submit: One

Approximate length
of manuscript: Not specified

Abstract requirement: None

Evaluation time: Two weeks

Payment: None

Additional
information: There is a cumulative index every ten years.

ASLA NEWSLETTER

(replaces *Arizona Librarian*, which ceased publication with the Winter 1971 issue)

Valencia Branch
Tucson Public Library
202 West Valencia Road
Tucson, Arizona 85706

Subscription: Free to members of Arizona State Library Association
Circulation: 850-900
Frequency: Monthly

Editor: Jeanne S. Bagby

Indexed in: Not specified

Description: Contains notices of interest to Arizona librarians; serves as the newsletter for the ASLA.

Contributors: ASLA members and officers

Style requirements: Not specified

Number of manuscript
copies to submit: Not specified

Approximate length
of manuscript: Not specified

Abstract requirement: Not specified

Evaluation time: Not specified

Payment: Not specified

ASLIB PROCEEDINGS

Association of Special Libraries and Information Sources
3 Belgrave Square
London S.W. 1, England

Subscription: £ 12; free to members
Circulation: 3,600
Frequency: Monthly

Editor: Not specified

Indexed in: Documentation Abstracts, Library Literature, Library and
Information Science Abstracts

Description: Provides information on the activities of **ASLIB**, which is the
English counterpart of the American Special Libraries
Association. Contains articles of interest to librarians within
the Association, on such topics as computers, documentation, indexing, and bibliographic control.

Contributors: Authorities in the field

Style requirements: Not specified

Number of manuscript
copies to submit: One

Approximate length
of manuscript: Up to 1,500 words

Abstract requirement: None

Evaluation time: Up to six weeks

Payment: None

ALABAMA LIBRARIAN

State Department of Education
Montgomery, Alabama 36104

Subscription: $3.00; free to members of the Alabama Library Association
Circulation: 750
Frequency: Quarterly

Editor: Luther E. Lee
Address: P.O. Box 6184
              Montgomery, Alabama 36106

Indexed in: Library Literature, Library and Information Science Abstracts

Description: Articles of interest to Alabama librarians, news of the
              association, addresses of conference speakers

Contributors: Mainly librarians

Style requirements: Not specified

Number of manuscript
copies to submit: One

Approximate length
of manuscript: Not specified

Abstract requirement: None

Evaluation time: Up to six weeks

Payment: None

Additional
information: This is the official publication of the Alabama
                          Library Association. Final date for submission of
                          material to be published is the first day of the
                          month preceding the month of publication.

AMERICAN ARCHIVIST

Society of American Archivists
National Archives
Washington, D.C. 20408

Subscription: $15.00; single issue, $3.75
Circulation: 2,400
Frequency: Quarterly

Editor: Edward Weldon

Indexed in: Library Literature, Library and Information Science Abstracts, PAIS, Archives

Description: Published by the Society of American Archivists. Emphasizes archives administration and history, records management, and historical editing.

Contributors: Authorities in the field; scope not limited to librarians

Style requirements: GPO; journal's own style sheet

Number of manuscript
copies to submit: Two

Approximate length
of manuscript: Generally 10 to 20 typed pages, but longer and shorter manuscripts are accepted

Abstract requirement: None

Evaluation time: Six weeks to two months

Payment: None

Additional
information: Occasionally French and Spanish articles are printed, with English summaries.

AMERICAN BOOK COLLECTOR

1822 School Street
Chicago, Illinois 60657

Subscription: $7.50
Circulation: 2,000
Frequency: Monthly from September to June

Editor: W. B. Thorsen

Indexed in: Abstracts of English Studies, Historical Abstracts, America: History and Life

Description: Of interest to book collectors but also to lay readers. Articles include checklists, book reviews, articles about authors, collections, bookbinders, etc.

Contributors: Librarians, bibliographers, book collectors, and members of the antiquarian book trade

Style requirements: *A Manual of Style* (University of Chicago Press)

Number of manuscript
copies to submit: One

Approximate length
of manuscript: 1,000 to 5,000 words

Abstract requirement: None

Evaluation time: One to two weeks

Payment: None

AMERICAN LIBRARIES
(formerly *ALA Bulletin*)

American Library Association
50 East Huron Street
Chicago, Illinois 60611

Subscription: $1.50 (included in membership dues); single issues, $1.50
Circulation: 38,000
Frequency: Monthly except for July-August issue

Editor: Gerald R. Shields

Indexed in: Readers' Guide to Periodical Literature, Education Index, Library Literature, Library and Information Science Abstracts, Current Contents

Description: Carries articles on current library services, interests, and development, and articles of general value to the profession. This is the official bulletin of the American Library Association.

Contributors: Primarily librarians

Style requirements: Not specified

Number of manuscript copies to submit: One

Approximate length of manuscript: Up to 6,000 words, but exceptions are made

Abstract requirement: None

Evaluation time: Up to eight weeks

Payment: None

Additional information: ". . . does not currently accept manuscripts as it is under budgetary restrictions which preclude the publication of feature material in 1973."

ARKANSAS LIBRARIES

Arkansas Library Commission
506½ Center Street
Little Rock, Arkansas 72201

Subscription: $5.00; free to members of the Arkansas Library Association
Circulation: Approximately 800
Frequency: Quarterly

Editor: LaNell Compton

Indexed in: Library Literature

Description: This is a joint publication of the state library association and the state library commission. Most articles are news items about libraries within the state.

Contributors: Arkansas librarians

Style requirements: Not specified

Number of manuscript
copies to submit: One

Approximate length
of manuscript: Under 1,000 words

Abstract requirement: None

Evaluation time: Up to three weeks

Payment: None

THE ASSISTANT LIBRARIAN: Journal of the Association of Assistant Librarians

Central Library
Manor Park Road
Sutton, Surrey, England

Subscription: Free to members
Circulation: 12,000
Frequency: Monthly

Editor: Bob Usherwood

Indexed in: Library Literature, Library and Information Science Abstracts

Description: Presents the opinions of younger members of the English library profession about traditional ideas and views. Articles reflect the "social responsibilities" of librarianship.

Contributors: Primarily librarians

Style requirements: Not specified

Number of manuscript
copies to submit: One

Approximate length
of manuscript: Up to 4,500 words

Abstract requirement: Useful, but not required

Evaluation time: Within two weeks

Payment: None

Additional
information: Illustrations should be supplied whenever possible. Copy date is the fifth of the month for inclusion in the next month's issue. Because of severe pressure on space, the month of publication will not be specified.

AUSTRALIAN LIBRARY JOURNAL

32 Belvoir Street
Surry Hills, NSW 2010
Australia

Subscription: A$12.50
Circulation: 6,800
Frequency: Monthly except January

Editor: W. L. Brown

Address: 9 Richardson Street
Essendon, Vic 3040
Australia

Indexed in: Library Literature, Library and Information Science Abstracts, Australian Public Affairs Information Service

Description: This is the official organ of the Library Association of Australia. "It endeavours to reflect and record the Australian library scene, to contribute to the solution of problems in the theory and practice of librarianship, and to represent Australian librarianship in Australia and overseas."

Contributors: Primarily staff members of Australian libraries

Style requirements: F. H. Collins, *Authors' and Printers' Dictionary* (Oxford University Press, 1965); H. Hart, *Hart's Rules for Compositors and Readers at the University Press, Oxford* (Oxford University Press, 1967); style sheet available on request.

Number of manuscript
copies to submit: Two

Approximate length
of manuscript: 3,000 words

Abstract requirement: Yes; not more than 100 words (UNESCO Standard)

Evaluation time: Two weeks

Payment: None, but 25 free offprints are supplied to each contributor

BAY STATE LIBRARIAN

Cary Memorial Library
1874 Massachusetts Avenue
Lexington, Massachusetts 02173

Subscription: $4.00; free to members
Circulation: 2,000
Frequency: Quarterly

Editor: Robert E. Cain

Indexed in: Library Literature

Description: Bulletin of the Massachusetts Library Association. Articles
               concern librarianship in Massachusetts or are otherwise
               related to aspects of Massachusetts.

Contributors: Primarily librarians

Style requirements: Not specified

Number of manuscript
copies to submit: One

Approximate length
of manuscript: 2,500 words

Abstract requirement: Recommended, but not required

Evaluation time: One month

Payment: None

BIBLIOGRAPHICAL SOCIETY OF AMERICA. PAPERS.

P.O. Box 397
Grand Central Station
New York, New York 10017

Subscription: $15.00
Circulation: 1,700
Frequency: Quarterly

Editor: William B. Todd
Address: 110 Parlin Hall
              University of Texas
              Austin, Texas 78712

Indexed in: Library Literature, Social Sciences and Humanities Index,
              MLA International Bibliography, Annual Bibliography of
              English Language and Literature

Description: Emphasizes analytical and historical bibliography, printing
              history, and related topics.

Contributors: Primarily librarians, bibliographers, and authors concerned
              with the field of literature.

Style requirements: *MLA Style Sheet*

Number of manuscript
copies to submit: One (return postage should be included)

Approximate length
of manuscript: 1,000 to 4,000 words for articles; 100 to 1,000 words
                       for notes

Abstract requirement: According to MLA specifications

Evaluation time: Four months

Payment: None

Additional
information: Accepted material is normally published 12 to 18
                       months after submission.

BODLEIAN LIBRARY RECORD

Bodleian Library
The University of Oxford
Oxford, OX1, 3BD
England

Subscription: $1.50, single issue
Circulation: 2,100
Frequency: At least once a year

Editor: Not specified

Indexed in: Library and Information Science Abstracts

Description: Articles on the Bodleian Library and its collections, and on research using materials in the collections. Most articles are of a bibliographic and historical nature.

Contributors: Scholars and bibliographers

Style requirements: Not specified

Number of manuscript
copies to submit: One

Approximate length
of manuscript: No set policy

Abstract requirement: Not specified

Evaluation time: Not specified

Payment: None

THE BOOKLIST
(formerly *Booklist and Subscription Books Bulletin*)

American Library Association
50 East Huron Street
Chicago, Illinois 60611

Subscription: $15.00
Circulation: 38,000
Frequency: Twice a month, September through July; once in August

Editor: Edna Vanek

Indexed in: Its own semi-annual cumulative index

Description: Reviews books, pamphlets, and audiovisual materials

Contributors: Not specified

Style requirements: Not specified

Number of manuscript
copies to submit: Not specified

Approximate length
of manuscript: Not specified

Abstract requirement: None

Evaluation time: Not specified

Payment: None

Additional
information: Because this is primarily a reviewing journal, most
of the above items are not applicable.

THE BOOKMARK

University of Idaho Library
Moscow, Idaho

Subscription: Free on request to faculty and selected academic libraries
Circulation: Not specified
Frequency: Quarterly

Editor: Richard J. Beck

Indexed in: Library Literature, Library and Information Science Abstracts

Description: A quarterly newsletter that does not solicit manuscripts from
               anyone outside the staff of *The Bookmark*. They may "re-
               print some articles with permission." Most of the articles
               relate to the University of Idaho Library.

Contributors: Staff members

Style requirements: Not specified

Number of manuscript
copies to submit: Not applicable

Approximate length
of manuscript: Not applicable

Abstract requirement: Not applicable

Evaluation time: Not applicable

Payment: None

BOOKS AND LIBRARIES

Kenneth Spencer Research Library
University of Kansas
Lawrence, Kansas 66044

Subscription: Free to all University of Kansas staff members and to
interested individuals; an exchange item for institutions
Circulation: 2,500
Frequency: Quarterly

Editor: Barbara Backus

Indexed in: Not specified

Description: Carries articles concerning the University of Kansas Libraries, whether scholarly or of general interest.

Contributors: Library staff and faculty

Style requirements: Not specified

Number of manuscript
copies to submit: One

Approximate length
of manuscripts: No set policy

Abstract requirement: None

Evaluation time: Not specified

Payment: None

Additional
information: This publication is rarely an outlet for authors outside the University of Kansas, except for pertinent library lectures, etc.

BRITISH COLUMBIA LIBRARY QUARTERLY

British Columbia Library Association
2425 Macdonald Street
Vancouver 8, British Columbia
Canada

Subscription: $7.00; free to members
Circulation: 600
Frequency: Quarterly

Editor: Bryan Bacon   Mari Stainsby

Address: Chief Librarian   5622 East Broadway
Burnaby Public Library   Burnaby, British Columbia
Burnaby 2, B.C.   Canada
Canada

Indexed in: Canadian Periodical Index, Library Literature, Library and Information Science Abstracts

Description: Carries articles of interest to librarians in the British Columbia Library Association. The range of the articles is broad and includes children's books, library usage, and fiction within the library context.

Contributors: Primarily librarians

Style requirements: Not specified

Number of manuscript
copies to submit: Not specified

Approximate length
of manuscript: Up to 3,000 words

Abstract requirement: None

Evaluation time: Up to six weeks

Payment: None

BULLETIN OF BIBLIOGRAPHY AND MAGAZINE NOTES

F. W. Faxon Company
15 Southwest Park
Westwood, Massachusetts 02090

Subscription:	$10.00; single issues, $4.00
Circulation:	1,200
Frequency:	Quarterly (index for the year included in last issue)

Editor: Arpie Demirjian

Indexed in: Library Literature, Library and Information Science Abstracts

Description: Bibliographies, checklists, research and reference studies, profiles, and record of new, changed, and ceased periodicals.

Contributors: Not primarily librarians

Style requirements: *MLA Style Sheet*

Number of manuscript
copies to submit: One

Approximate length
of manuscript: Up to 60 pages

Abstract requirement: None

Evaluation time: Approximately six weeks

Payment: None

Additional
information: "Institutional affiliation or academic credentials should be indicated in initial correspondence."

BULLETIN OF THE CENTER FOR CHILDREN'S BOOKS

1100 East 57th Street
Chicago, Illinois 60637

Subscription: $8.00
Circulation: 10,500
Frequency: 11 issues per year

Editor: Zena Sutherland

Indexed in: Not specified

Description: A book selection aid which contains Zena Sutherland's
              reviews of current books for children and young people.
              There are no articles.

Contributors: No outside contributors are used.

Style requirements: Not applicable

Number of manuscript
copies to submit: Not applicable

Approximate length
of manuscript: Not applicable

Abstract requirement: Not applicable

Evaluation time: Not applicable

Payment: Not applicable

BULLETIN OF THE MEDICAL LIBRARY ASSOCIATION

Countway Library of Medicine
10 Shattuck Street
Boston, Massachusetts 02115

Subscription: $20.00
Circulation: 3,000
Frequency: Quarterly

Editor: Harold Bloomquist

Indexed in: Cumulative Index to Nursing Literature, Documentation Abstracts, Hospital Literature Index, Index Medicus, Index to Dental Literature, International Nursing Index, International Pharmaceutical Abstracts, Library and Information Science Abstracts, Library Literature, Science Citation Index

Description: A publication of the Medical Library Association; concerned with medical bibliography and librarianship

Contributors: Primarily librarians

Style requirements: *A Manual of Style* (University of Chicago Press); *Webster's Third New International Dictionary*

Number of manuscript
copies to submit: Three

Approximate length
of manuscript: Up to 25 pages

Abstract requirement: "An abstract not exceeding 150 words should be included on a separate sheet; it should state the paper's major points rather than merely indicate the topics discussed."

Evaluation time: Two to four weeks

Payment: None

Additional
information: A section called "Editorial Policies for the Guidance of Authors" is at the front of each issue.

BULLETIN OF THE NEW YORK PUBLIC LIBRARY

New York Public Library
Fifth Avenue and 42nd Street
New York, New York 10018

Subscription: $7.50
Circulation: 2,200
Frequency: Annual as of 1972; formerly 10 issues per year

Editor: David V. Erdman

Indexed in: PMLA Index, PAIS, Abstracts of English Studies, Bibliographic Index

Description: Contains bibliographies and checklists on various topics, including history, literature, the arts, science and technology, and economics. Encourages studies using the library's collection. Articles must relate in some way to the library's holdings.

Contributors: Primarily librarians

Style requirements: *MLA Style Sheet*; consult recent issues, however, for certain punctuation modifications.

Number of manuscript
copies to submit: One

Approximate length
of manuscript: No set policy

Abstract requirement: 100 to 150 words

Evaluation time: Two to three months

Payment: None

Additional
information: If manuscripts are lengthy, the editor will consider separate publication. According to Katz's *Magazines for Libraries* (1972), "January 1, 1972, the publisher announced that the *Bulletin* would be suspended for six months. In the hopes that it will be continued when money is again available . . . " Concerned authors should inquire before submitting a manuscript.

CALIFORNIA LIBRARIAN

California Library Association
717 K Street
Sacramento, California 95814

Subscription: $10.00; free to members
Circulation: 4,500
Frequency: Quarterly

Editor: Morris Polan

Address: John F. Kennedy Memorial Library
               California State College at Los Angeles
               5151 State College Drive
               Los Angeles, California 90032

Indexed in: Library Literature, Library and Information Science
               Abstracts

Description: Official publication of California Library Association. It con-
               tains articles of interest to librarians in all types of libraries.

Contributors: Primarily librarians

Style requirements: Not specified

Number of manuscript
copies to submit: One

Approximate length
of manuscript: Up to 2,000 words

Abstract requirement: Abstract of up to 150 words required

Evaluation time: Up to six weeks

Payment: None

CALIFORNIA SCHOOL LIBRARIES

P.O. Box 1277
Burlingame, California 94010

Subscription: $5.00; free to members
Circulation: 2,500
Frequency: Quarterly

Editor: Chase Dane

Indexed in: Library Literature

Description: This is the official publication of the California Association of School Libraries. It carries articles on the philosophy of school librarianship and bibliography of multi-media materials, and is "especially interested in articles describing actual and model school library programs throughout the State."

Contributors: Mainly librarians and teachers

Style requirements: *MLA Style Sheet*

Number of manuscript
copies to submit: One

Approximate length
of manuscript: Six pages

Abstract requirement: None

Evaluation time: One to two months

Payment: None

CANADIAN LIBRARY JOURNAL
(formerly *Canadian Libraries*)

Canadian Library Association
151 Sparks Street
Ottawa, Ontario K1P 5E3
Canada

Subscription: $10.00; single issue, $2.00
Circulation: Approximately 5,000
Frequency: Bimonthly

Editor: Louise Rickenbacker

Indexed in: Canadian Periodical Index, Library Literature, Library and
                  Information Science Abstracts

Description: Publication of the Canadian Library Association. Contains
                  articles on libraries and librarianship; coverage is international
                  rather than limited to Canadian aspects.

Contributors: Primarily librarians

Style requirements: Not specified

Number of manuscript
copies to submit: Two

Approximate length
of manuscript: 2,500 words

Abstract requirement: Submit before sending the manuscript

Evaluation time: Up to six weeks

Payment: None

Additional
information: If possible, include black and white glossy photo-
                             graphs for illustration.

CANADIAN NOTES AND QUERIES

Bernard Amtmann, Inc.
Montreal, Canada

Subscription: Limited free distribution
Circulation: 500
Frequency: Irregular (two or three per year)

Editor: William F. E. Morley
Address: Douglas Library
Queen's University
Kingston, Ontario, Canada

Indexed in: Not specified

Description: Consists of questions and replies, and notes on problems that arise in research and investigation. Serves as a means of exchanging information regarding research.

Contributors: Scholars and students in Canadian studies.

Style requirements: *Scholarly Reporting in the Humanities* (University of Toronto Press)

Number of manuscript
copies to submit: One

Approximate length
of manuscripts: 100 words

Abstract requirement: None

Evaluation time: Within one week

Payment: None

CATHOLIC LIBRARY WORLD

The Catholic Library Association
461 West Lancaster Avenue
Haverford, Pennsylvania 19041

Subscription: $10.00; free to members
Circulation: 4,250
Frequency: Monthly from September through April; bimonthly in
              May-June and July-August

Editor: Jane F. Hindman

Indexed in: Catholic Periodical and Literature Index, Library and Infor-
              mation Science Abstracts, Library Literature, Book Review
              Digest

Description: Official bulletin of the Catholic Library Association. Contains
              bibliographies, articles on innovative ideas in libraries and
              librarianship, and news of the Association.

Contributors: Not primarily librarians

Style requirements: Not specified

Number of manuscript
copies to submit: One

Approximate length
of manuscript: 2,000 to 2,500 words

Abstract requirement: None

Evaluation time: Two weeks

Payment: None

Additional
information: The manuscript will be returned promptly if not
                       accepted.

COLBY LIBRARY QUARTERLY

Colby College Library
Waterville, Maine 04901

Subscription: $3.00
Circulation: 700
Frequency: Quarterly

Editor: Richard Cary

Indexed in: Not specified

Description: Carries articles about authors represented in the special
              collections of the Colby College Library; the articles are of
              particular interest to rare book collectors.

Contributors: Mainly faculty members

Style requirements: Not specified

Number of manuscript
copies to submit: One

Approximate length
of manuscript: Up to 25 pages

Abstract requirement: 200 words, for MLA Abstracts

Evaluation time: Three weeks

Payment: None

COLLEGE AND RESEARCH LIBRARIES

Association of College and Research Libraries
Division of ALA
50 East Huron Street
Chicago, Illinois 60611

Subscription: $10.00; free to members
Circulation: 18,000
Frequency: 17 issues per year (bimonthly, plus 11 news issues)

Editor: Richard M. Dougherty

Address: University Librarian
University of California
Berkeley, California 94720

Indexed in: Library Literature, Library and Information Science Abstracts, Science Citation Index, Book Review Index, Current Contents, Current Index to Journals in Education, Historical Abstracts, America: History and Life

Description: Stresses trends, developments, and problems common to the field of academic and research librarianship.

Contributors: Primarily librarians

Style requirements: *A Manual of Style* (University of Chicago Press)

Number of manuscript
copies to submit: One

Approximate length
of manuscript: 1,800 to 4,000 words; occasionally, up to 10,000 words

Abstract requirement: Required (75 to 100 words)

Evaluation time: Up to six weeks

Payment: None

Additional
information: There is a tremendous backlog of manuscripts for publication.

COLORADO ACADEMIC LIBRARY

Norlin Library 148
University of Colorado
Boulder, Colorado 80302

Subscription: $3.75; free to members of College and University Division of
the Colorado Library Association

Circulation: 400

Frequency: Quarterly

Editor: Ruth Carol Cushman and Joseph M. Mapes

Indexed in: Library Literature

Description: Carries articles and news items of interest to academic
librarians in Colorado.

Contributors: Academic librarians interested in the problems and philosophy
of academic librarianship.

Style requirements: *MLA Style Sheet*

Number of manuscript
copies to submit: One

Approximate length
of manuscript: Two to eight typewritten pages

Abstract requirement: None

Evelution time: Three to four weeks

Payment: None

COLUMBIA LIBRARY COLUMNS

Friends of the Columbia Libraries
535 West 114th Street
New York, New York 10027

Subscription: $6.00
Circulation: 800
Frequency: Three issues per year

Editor: Dallas Pratt

Indexed in: Library Literature

Description: Articles relate primarily to the collection at the Columbia
              libraries. They are generally of a bibliographic and literary
              nature.

Contributors: Only solicited manuscripts are published.

Style requirements: Not applicable

Number of manuscript
copies to submit: Not applicable

Approximate length
of manuscript: Not applicable

Abstract requirement: Not applicable

Evaluation time: Not applicable

Payment: Not applicable

CONNECTICUT LIBRARIES
(formerly *Connecticut Library Association News and Views*)

New Haven Free Public Library
133 Elm Street
New Haven, Connecticut 06510

Subscription: $5.00; free to members
Circulation: Controlled
Frequency: Quarterly

Editor: Meredith Bloss

Indexed in: Library Literature

Description: Contains articles of interest to Connecticut libraries

Contributors: Primarily librarians

Style requirements: Manual available on request

Number of manuscript
copies to submit: One

Approximate length
of manuscript: Not specified

Abstract requirement: None

Evaluation time: Not specified

Payment: None

THE CRAB: Newsletter of the Maryland Library Association

Maryland Library Association
115 West Franklin Street
Baltimore, Maryland 21201

Subscription: $3.00; free to members
Circulation: 700
Frequency: Bimonthly

Editor: Pamela Bluh

Indexed in: Not specified

Description: Contains news of the Maryland Library Association, its divisions, and its special committees, as well as articles of interest to librarians in Maryland and in neighboring states.

Contributors: Librarians and members of the MLA Editorial Committee

Style requirements: Not specified

Number of manuscript
copies to submit: One

Approximate length
of manuscript: No set policy

Abstract requirement: None

Evaluation time: Within two weeks

Payment: None

Additional
information: Editorship changes each year.

DARTMOUTH COLLEGE LIBRARY BULLETIN

Dartmouth College Library
115 Baker Library
Hanover, New Hampshire 03755

Subscription: Free
Circulation: 1,790
Frequency: Twice a year

Editor: Theresa Blake and Virginia L. Close

Indexed in: Library Literature

Description: "A journal aimed at making the faculty and students more aware of the resources of the library."

Contributors: Faculty, library staff, and users of the Dartmouth College Library. Manuscripts from outside contributors are not solicited.

Style requirements: Not applicable

Number of manuscript
copies to submit: One

Approximate length
of manuscript: Six pages

Abstract requirement: None

Evaluation time: No set policy

Payment: None

DREXEL LIBRARY QUARTERLY

Graduate School of Library Science
Drexel University
Philadelphia, Pennsylvania 19104

Subscription: $10.00; single issue, $3.00
Circulation: Approximately 1,000
Frequency: Quarterly

Editor: Jane F. Spivack

Indexed in: Library Literature, Library and Information Science
Abstracts, PAIS, Vertical File Index, Book Review Index,
Current Contents, Current Index to Journals in Education,
Library and Information Science Abstracts

Description: Emphasizes scholarly aspects of librarianship. Each issue
treats a single subject from various points of view, usually
under the editorship of a specialist in the particular field.
Articles are solicited by the issue editor, from experts in
the field under study.

Contributors: Primarily librarians and information scientists

Style requirements: *A Manual of Style* (University of Chicago Press);
GPO *Style Manual*; Turabian's *Manual* . . .

Number of manuscript
copies to submit: Two

Approximate length
of manuscript: 10 to 15 typed pages

Abstract requirement: None

Evelution time: Not specified

Payment: Complimentary copies only

Additional
information: Ideas for an issue will be considered, but individual
articles are not accepted. Issues are planned six
months to a year in advance.

EDUCATION LIBRARIES BULLETIN

University of London
Institute of Education Library
11-13 Ridgmount Street
London, WC1E 7AH, England

Subscription: $3.25
Circulation: 700
Frequency: Quarterly

Editor: Michael Humby

Indexed in: Library and Information Science Abstracts, British Education
              Index, Current Contents/Behavioral, Social and Educational
              Sciences

Description: Contains articles on the British educational system and the
              British concept of education libraries

Contributors: Primarily educators and librarians

Style requirements: None specified

Number of manuscript
copies to submit: One

Approximate length
of manuscript: Up to 2,000 words

Abstract requirement: None

Evaluation time: Up to eight weeks

Payment: None

FILM LIBRARY QUARTERLY

Box 348, Radio City Station
New York, New York 10019

Subscription: $10.00
Circulation: 2,126
Frequency: Quarterly

Editor: William Sloan

Address: Donnell Library
          20 West 53rd Street
          New York, New York 10019

Indexed in: Library Literature

Description: Articles and reviews on non-print media materials, equipment, and services in public libraries and similar public, non-profit agencies, but not in schools.

Contributors: Librarians and library educators, filmmakers and distributors, community service personnel

Style requirements: Furnished on request

Number of manuscript
copies to submit: One

Approximate length
of manuscript: Eight to ten typed pages

Abstract requirement: None; however, contributors should submit outline to editor.

Evaluation time: Three weeks

Payment: None

FLORIDA LIBRARIES

Florida Library Association
3018 N.W. First Avenue
Gainesville, Florida 32601

Subscription: $5.00; free to members
Circulation: Not specified
Frequency: Quarterly

Editor: Lu Alice Sands

Indexed in: Library Literature

Description: Carries articles about technical aspects of librarianship,
               authors, and library history.

Contributors: Primarily librarians

Style requirements: Not specified

Number of manuscript
copies to submit: One

Approximate length
of manuscript: 1,500 to 3,000 words

Abstract requirement: None

Evaluation time: Approximately three months

Payment: None

GEORGIA LIBRARIAN

School Library Services Unit
State Department of Education
Atlanta, Georgia

Subscription: $5.00; free to members
Circulation: Approximately 1,200
Frequency: Semi-annual

Editor: Grace Hightower

Indexed in: Library Literature

Description: In general manuscripts are solicited on the basis of their interest to Georgia librarians. Manuscripts from out-of-state librarians are sometimes used if they have implications for libraries in Georgia.

Contributors: Librarians and educators

Style requirements: Not specified

Number of manuscript
copies to submit: One

Approximate length
of manuscript: 12 to 14 pages

Abstract requirement: None required, but it is suggested that an abstract be submitted before the manuscript itself.

Evelution time: No set policy; however, all mansucripts should be in the editor's hands at least six months before publication date.

Payment: Complimentary copies only

Additional
information: As a general rule, articles are informal, rather than highly structured.

HARVARD LIBRARIAN

Harvard University Library
Cambridge, Massachusetts 02138

Subscription: Free
Circulation: 2,500
Frequency: Bimonthly

Editor: Robert R. Walsh, Asst. Univ. Librarian for Building Planning

Address Widener Library 182
Harvard University
Cambridge, Massachusetts 02138

Indexed in: Not specified

Description: Provides news of the Harvard University Library for faculty, alumni, friends, other libraries, and university administrative offices

Contributors: Members of the Harvard University Library staff. Occasionally other interested individuals are invited to contribute articles.

Style requirements: Not specified

Number of manuscript
copies to submit: One

Approximate length
of manuscripts: No set policy

Abstract requirement: None

Evaluation time: Not applicable

Payment: None

Additional
information: Unsolicited manuscripts are not encouraged.

HARVARD LIBRARY BULLETIN

Harvard University
505 Lamont Library
Cambridge, Massachusetts 02138

Subscription: $15.00
Circulation: 1,700
Frequency: Quarterly

Editor: Edwin E. Williams

Indexed in: Library Literature

Description: Contains articles on Harvard libraries and their collections, on research using materials in these collections, and on research libraries in general.

Contributors: Researchers who use Harvard libraries or who write about them.

Style requirements: *MLA Style Sheet*. Footnotes should be numbered consecutively and typed (double-spaced) on a separate sheet at the end of the manuscript. Entire manuscript should be double-spaced.

Number of manuscript
copies to submit: One

Approximate length
of manuscript: Six to thirty pages

Abstract requirement: None

Evaluation time: Two weeks

Payment: None; however, 50 free offprints are supplied to each contributor

Additional
information: Return postage should accompany the manuscript.

HAWAII LIBRARY ASSOCIATION JOURNAL

Hawaii Library Association
P.O. Box 3941
Honolulu, Hawaii 96812

Subscription: $3.00; free to members
Circulation: 600
Frequency: Semi-annual

Editor: Linda Engelberg

Indexed in: Library Literature, Library and Information Science
              Abstracts

Description: Contains articles on libraries and library-related topics that
              are pertinent to Hawaii and the Pacific area.

Contributors: Librarians in Hawaii

Style requirements: Articles should be typewritten and double-spaced;
                      otherwise not specified

Number of manuscript
copies to submit: One

Approximate length
of mansucripts: 1,500 to 3,000 words

Abstract requirement: None

Evaluation time: One to four weeks

Payment: None

Additional
information: Manuscripts should be submitted four weeks before
                      the scheduled date of publication.

HERALD OF LIBRARY SCIENCE

Editor and Publisher
C 1
Banaras Hindu University
Varanasi 5, India

Subscription: $8.00
Circulation: Not specified
Frequency: Quarterly

Editor: P. N. Kaula

Indexed in: Library Literature, Library and Information Science Abstracts, Information Science Abstracts

Description: Articles pertaining to any aspect of librarianship

Contributors: Primarily librarians

Style requirements: Not specified

Number of manuscript
copies to submit: One

Approximate length
of manuscript: No set policy

Abstract requirement: Required

Evaluation time: Two to three weeks

Payment: None

Additional
information: If informed in advance of a possible topic, the editors can give a considered opinion as to whether or not the subject would be suitable.

THE HORN BOOK MAGAZINE

The Horn Book, Inc.
585 Boylston Street
Boston, Massachusetts 02116

Subscription: $7.50
Circulation: 27,500
Frequency: Bimonthly

Editor: Paul Heins

Indexed in: Readers' Guide to Periodical Literature, Book Review
               Digest, Book Review Index

Description: Articles on children's books and pleasure reading in the
               United States and abroad

Contributors: Primarily librarians and teachers

Style requirements: Manuscripts should be triple-spaced

Number of manuscript
copies to submit: One

Approximate length
of manuscript: Up to 2,000 words

Abstract requirement: None

Evaluation time: Up to six weeks

Payment: One cent per word; payment is within 30 days
                       after publication.

Additional
information: Poetry—traditional, contemporary, light verse—is
                       published at $10.00 per page.

HUNTINGTON LIBRARY QUARTERLY: A Journal for the History and Interpretation of English and American Civilization

Henry E. Huntington Library and Art Gallery
San Marino, California 91108

Subscription: $7.50
Circulation: 1,300
Frequency: Quarterly

Editor: John M. Steadman

Indexed in: Abstracts of English Studies

Description: This is a research journal rather than a library bulletin. It contains articles on English history and literature (with an emphasis on the English Renaissance through the eighteenth century), on American history and literature (emphasizing the Colonial period, the Civil War, and Western Americana), and on British art history (emphasizing the eighteenth and early nineteenth centuries).

Contributors: Primarily scholars in the above areas rather than librarians.

Style requirements: Format rules are listed in the November issue.

Number of manuscript
copies to submit: One

Approximate length
of manuscripts: 15 to 30 pages

Abstract requirement: Required; included in the MLA Abstract

Evaluation time: Four to six weeks

Payment: None

INSPEL: International Journal of Special Libraries

Special Libraries Section
National Housing Center
1625 L Street N.W.
Washington, D.C. 20036

Subscription: $4.00
Circulation: 400
Frequency: Quarterly

Editor: Karl A. Baer

Indexed in: Library Literature, Library and Information Science
               Abstracts

Description: Contains articles in English, French, German, and Russian,
               which relate to special libraries on an international level.

Contributors: Primarily librarians

Style requirements: Not specified

Number of manuscaript
copies to submit: One

Approximate length
of manuscripts: As brief as possible

Abstract requirement: None

Evaluation time: No set policy

Payment: Yes, but not specified

IPLO QUARTERLY

Institute of Professional Librarians of Ontario
17 Inkerman Street
Toronto 5, Ontario
Canada

Subscription: $10.00; free to members
Circulation: Not specified
Frequency: Quarterly

Editor: Les Fowlie (Acting Editor)

Indexed in: Library Literature

Description: Contains articles covering all aspects of librarianship and bibliography ; not limited to articles of interest to the Toronto region.

Contributors: Primarily librarians

Style requirements: Not specified

Number of manuscript
copies to submit: One

Approximate length
of manuscript: Up to 3,000 words

Abstract requirement: None

Evaluation time: Not specified

Payment: None

IDAHO LIBRARIAN

University of Idaho Library
Moscow, Idaho 83843

Subscription: $5.00; free to members of the Idaho Library Association
Circulation: 1,000
Frequency: Quarterly

Editor: Stanley A. Shepard

Indexed in: Library Literature

Description: Contains informational, educational, do-it-yourself articles,
               in addition to news of interest to Idaho librarians.

Contributors: Primarily librarians

Style requirements: Not specified

Number of manuscript
copies to submit: One

Approximate length
of manuscript: Not over six pages

Abstract requirement: None

Evaluation time: One to two weeks

Payment: None

ILLINOIS LIBRARIES

Publications Unit
Illinois State Library
Office of the Secretary of State
Springfield, Illinois 62706

Subscription: Free to Illinois libraries
Circulation: 8,500
Frequency: Monthly from September through June

Editor: Irma Bostian

Indexed in: Library Literature

Description: Because each issue is devoted to a particular subject (such as
               library cooperation, school libraries, etc.), most manuscripts
               are solicited. There is one miscellaneous issue each year.

Contributors: Primarily librarians

Style requirements: Not specified

Number of manuscript
copies to submit: One

Approximate length
of manuscript: Five to twenty pages

Abstract requirement: None

Evaluation time: Varies according to subject and length of manu-
                         script; up to two months

Payment: None

THE INDIAN LIBRARIAN: A Magazine on Libraries and Literature

233 Model Town
Jullundur City—3
India

Subscription: $8.00
Circulation: Over 12,000
Frequency: Quarterly

Editor: Sant Ram Bhatia

Indexed in: Library Literature, Library and Information Science
               Abstracts, Current Contents, Guide to Indian Periodical
               Literature

Description: Contains articles on Indian librarianship, librarianship in
               general, and related topics

Contributors: Primarily librarians (Indian, American, Canadian, Russian,
              and others)

Style requirements: Not specified

Number of manuscript
copies to submit: One

Approximate length
of manuscript: 3,000 to 5,000 words

Abstract requirement: None

Evaluation time: Two to three months

Payment: Usually none

Additional
information: Includes major articles and news of the library
                           field, news of forthcoming events, activities of library
                           associations, new appointments, reviews of library
                           literature as well as of technical, medical, and
                           scientific books, paperbacks, religious books, and
                           juvenile books.

INDIAN LIBRARY ASSOCIATION BULLETIN
(supersedes *Indian Library Association Journal*)

Indian Library Association
Delhi Public Library
S. P. Mukerjee Marg
Delhi 6, India

Subscription: $6.00; free to members
Circulation: 1,750
Frequency: Quarterly

Editor: B. L. Bharadwaja

Indexed in: Library and Information Science Abstracts, Library Litera-
               ture

Description: Contains articles on all phases of librarianship, library
               science, and library development

Contributors: Primarily librarians

Style requirements: Not specified

Number of manuscript
copies to submit: One

Approximate length
of manuscripts: No set policy

Abstract requirement: Required

Evaluation time: Two months

Payment: None

INFORMATION SCIENCES: An International Journal

American Elsevier Publishing Company, Inc.
52 Vanderbilt Avenue
New York, New York 10017

Subscription: $30.00
Circulation: Not specified
Frequency: Quarterly

Editor: John M. Richardson

Address: North American Rockwell Corporation
             Science Center, Aerospace and Systems Group
             1049 Camino Dos Rios
             Thousand Oaks, California 91360

Indexed in: Engineering Index, Mathematical Reviews, Computer
             Abstracts, Chemical Abstracts, Science Abstracts

Description: "Publishes carefully selected papers of both research and
             expository type devoted to theoretical and experimental
             results in the information sciences."

Contributors: Anyone working in one of the fields of information science:
             communications, signal recognition theory, estimation
             theory, etc.

Style requirements: *Style Manual for Guidance in the Preparation of
                      Papers* (American Institute of Physics); "Information
                      for Authors" on outside back cover of journal

Number of manuscript
copies to submit: Two

Approximate length
of manuscript: 15 to 20 typed pages

Abstract requirement: Required

Evaluation time: One to three months

Payment: 50 reprints

Additional
information: Manuscripts may be submitted to any of the members
                      of the editorial board or to the editor-in-chief. Manu-
                      scripts may be in English, French, German, or
                      Spanish.

INFORMATION STORAGE AND RETRIEVAL: Theory and Practice

Pergamon Press, Inc.
Maxwell House, Fairview Park
Elmsford, New York 10523

Subscription: $40.00
Circulation: Not specified
Frequency: Bimonthly

Editor: Bernard H. Fry

Address: Dean, Graduate Library School
Indiana University
Bloomington, Indiana 47401

Indexed in: Library and Information Science Abstracts, Mathematical
Reviews

Description: Contributions must be in English, French, German, or Italian.
This international journal discusses information storage and
retrieval as part of the total communications process.

Contributors: Primarily librarians and information scientists

Style requirements: "Information for Contributors" will be sent on
request; the inside back cover of the journal also
contains stylistic information.

Number of manuscript
copies to submit: Two

Approximate length
of manuscript: Up to 2,000 words

Abstract requirement: Required

Evaluation time: Up to eight weeks

Payment: There is a voluntary page charge of $35.00 per page. Pay-
ment or non-payment of the charge, however, will not
affect acceptance of a manuscript for publication.

Additional
information: Manuscripts may be sent to the assistant and regional
editors as well as to the editor-in-chief; names and
addresses are listed on the inside front cover of the
journal.

INTERNATIONAL LIBRARY REVIEW

Academic Press, Ltd.   Academic Press, Inc.
24-28 Oval Road   111 Fifth Avenue
London NW 1, England   New York, New York 10003

Subscription: $30.00
Circulation: Unavailable
Frequency: Quarterly

Editor: George Chandler

Address: 23 Dowsefield Lane
     Liverpool, England L18 3JG

Indexed in: Library Literature, Library and Information Science Abstracts

Description: "Deals with all aspects of progress and research in inter-
     national and comparative librarianship, documentation, and
     information retrieval in national, public, universal, and
     special libraries."

Contributors: Librarians and educators

Style requirements: "Information for Authors" is printed on the
          inside back cover of each issue.

Number of manuscript
copies to submit: Two

Approximate length
of manuscript: 15 to 20 typed pages

Abstract requirement: None

Evaluation time: Not specified

Payment: 50 free reprints

IOWA LIBRARY QUARTERLY

Iowa State Traveling Library
Historical Building
Des Moines, Iowa 50319

Subscription: Free to Iowa libraries
Circulation: 14,000
Frequency: Quarterly

Editor: Florence Stiles

Indexed in: Library Literature

Description: Contains articles pertaining to Iowa libraries and their programs.

Contributors: Librarians in Iowa

Style requirements: Not specified

Number of manuscript
copies to submit: One

Approximate length
of manuscript: Shorter ones are preferred

Abstract requirement: None

Evaluation time: Two to three weeks

Payment: None

JOURNAL OF DOCUMENTATION: Devoted to the Recording, Organization and Dissemination of Specialized Knowledge

ASLIB
2 Belgrave Square
London, WW1, England

Subscription: £10; £1.80 to members of ASLIB
Circulation: 3,500
Frequency: Quarterly

Editor: H. Coblans

Indexed in: Library Literature, Library and Information Science Abstracts, Chemical Abstracts, Information Science Abstracts

Description: Articles deal with methods of presenting information, including translations, abstracts, indexes and other bibliographic aids; the organization and distribution of such literature through learned societies and libraries; and the recording, organization, and classification and dissemination of information.

Contributors: Primarily librarians and scholars

Style requirements: Footnotes should be avoided whenever possible. If included, they should come at the end of the manuscript and should follow P. G. Burbridge's *Notes and References* (1952). For additional information as to style, consult the inside front cover of the journal.

Number of manuscript
copies to submit: Two

Approximate length
of manuscript: 5,000 words

Abstract requirement: Required; up to 200 words

Evaluation time: Six to eight weeks

Payment: Yes, plus 25 free copies

JOURNAL OF EDUCATION FOR LIBRARIANSHIP

Publications Office
471 Park Lane
State College, Pennsylvania 16801

Subscription: $8.00
Circulation: 1,500
Frequency: Quarterly

Editor: Norman Horrocks

Address: School of Library Service
               Dalhousie University
               Halifax, N.S., Canada

Indexed in: Library Literature, Library and Information Science
               Abstracts

Description: Official publication of the Association of American Library
               Schools. Pertains to library education and is of particular
               interest to library science educators.

Contributors: Primarily library educators, but also practicing librarians

Style requirements: Not specified

Number of manuscript
copies to submit: One

Approximate length
of manuscript: 1,000 to 3,000 words

Abstract requirement: None

Evaluation time: Up to six weeks

Payment: None

Additional
information: This is the official organ of the Association of
                       American Library Schools.

JOURNAL OF LIBRARIANSHIP: Quarterly of the Library Association

The Library Association
7 Ridgmount Street
London, WC1E 7AE
England

Subscription: £5; $12.50 in the United States
Circulation: Not specified
Frequency: Quarterly

Editor: S. J. Butcher

Indexed in: Library Literature

Description: Covers the whole field of librarianship and documentation, both in the United Kingdom and abroad. Articles should make a contribution to published knowledge in the field and should be based on research and investigation.

Contributors: Primarily librarians

Style requirements: "Notes to Contributors" is the journal's style manual; footnotes should be avoided.

Number of manuscript
copies to submit: Two

Approximate length
of manuscript: 4,000 to 7,000 words

Abstract requirement: Required (50 to 100 words)

Evaluation time: Three to six months

Payment: Normally none, but exceptions are made.

Additional
information: Authors must submit brief biographical notes of not more than 50 words. Prior to submission of the manuscript, contributors may offer a detailed synopsis for evaluation.

JOURNAL OF LIBRARY AUTOMATION

General Library
University of California
Berkeley, California 94720

Subscription: $15.00; free to members
Circulation: 6,000
Frequency: Quarterly

Editor: Susan Martin

Indexed in: Current Contents, Current Index to Journals in Education,
               Library Literature, Chemical Abstracts, Information Science
               Abstracts, Library and Information Science Abstracts

Description: American Library Association scholarly papers and technical
               reports with findings not previously published. Research
               and development in library automation, the history and
               teaching of information science, systems and designs in
               libraries.

Contributors: Librarians and library automation educators concerned with
               research and information science.

Style requirements: *A Manual of Style* (University of Chicago Press)

Number of manuscript
copies to submit: Two

Approximate length
of manuscript: 10 to 30 pages, but longer manuscripts will also be
                        considered

Abstract requirement: Required (150 words)

Evaluation time: Six to eight tweeks

Payment: Complimentary copies only; reprints at fees

Additional
information: Brief news items should be sent to Donald L. Bosseau,
                        Director of Libraries, University of Texas, El Paso,
                        Texas 79968. Any tables, figures, printouts, or
                        charts should be submitted in the original rather
                        than as photocopies.

JOURNAL OF LIBRARY HISTORY: Philosophy and Comparative Librarianship

School of Library Science
Florida State University
Tallahassee, Florida 32306

Subscription: $12.50
Circulation: 1,300
Frequency: Quarterly

Editor: Harold Goldstein

Indexed in: Library Literature, Book Review Index, America: History and Life, Historical Abstracts, Library and Information Science Abstracts, and Current Contents

Description: Carries scholarly and readable articles on the history of librarianship, the philosophy of librarianship, comparative librarianship, and the state of the art of library history.

Contributors: Not specified

Style requirements: Turabian's *Manual* . . .

Number of manuscript
copies to submit: Two

Approximate length
of manuscript: Research studies, 2,000 to 5,000 words (longer in exceptional cases); essays, 2,000 to 3,000 words; vignettes, up to 1,000 words; previously unpublished documents, up to 3,000 words.

Abstract requirement: None

Evaluation time: Three to five months

Payment: None. An annual award ($100 plus a citation) recognizes the most outstanding manuscript of the preceding calendar year.

Additional
information: Bibliographies are also published. Rejected manuscripts are criticized, with indications as to whether the manuscript should be rewritten and submitted again.

JOURNAL OF THE AMERICAN SOCIETY FOR INFORMATION SCIENCE   (formerly *American Documentation*)

American Society for Information Science
Suite 804
1140 Connecticut Avenue, N.W.
Washington, D.C. 20036

Subscription: $35.00; free to members
Circulation: Approximately 3,600
Frequency: Bimonthly

Editor: Arthur W. Elias

Address: Journal of the American Society for Information Science
              Informatics
              6000 Executive Boulevard
              Rockville, Maryland 20852

Indexed in: Chemical Abstracts, Current Contents, Information Science
              Abstracts, Library Literature, Library and Information
              Science Abstracts, Science Citation Index

Description: Scholar journal on the research and philosophical aspects of
              documentation

Contributors: Librarians and subject specialists

Style requirements: "Style Manual for Biological Journals," published by
                      the American Institute of Biological Sciences (1964),
                      will be sent on request. Also, the March-April 1973
                      issue contains "Instructions to Authors." Author's
                      surname should be on every page (top right corner).

Number of manuscript
copies to submit: Three

Approximate length
of manuscript: No set policy

Abstract requirement: Required (up to 200 words). Should indicate scope,
                      methods, results, and conclusions.

Evaluation time: One to three months

Payment: None

KANSAS LIBRARY BULLETIN

Kansas State Library
State Capitol Building
801 Harrison
Topeka, Kansas 66612

Subscription: Free to Kansas libraries
Circulation: Approximately 4,000
Frequency: Quarterly

Editor: Cass Peterson

Indexed in: Library Literature

Description: Because the audience consists of Kansas librarians and library trustees, technical material must be simplified enough so that people with little library training can understand it. Articles describe new services, public relations programs, and common library problems, with the aim of assisting small public libraries within the state.

Contributors: Librarians, library trustees, and patrons

Style requirements: Not specified; copy is edited before publication to conform to the journal's style

Number of manuscript
copies to submit: One

Approximate length
of manuscript: No set policy

Abstract requirement: None

Evaluation time: Two weeks

Payment: None

KENTUCKY LIBRARY ASSOCIATION BULLETIN

University of Kentucky
College of Library Science
Lexington, Kentucky 40506

Subscription: $6.00; free to members of the Kentucky Library Association
Circulation: 1,000 (controlled)
Frequency: Quarterly

Editor: Charles Evans

Indexed in: Library Literature

Description: Contains material pertaining to Kentucky authors or of
              interest to Kentucky librarians.

Contributors: Primarily Kentucky librarians

Style requirements: Not specified

Number of manuscript
copies to submit: One

Approximate length
of manuscript: No set policy

Abstract requirement: None

Evaluation time: Not specified

Payment: None

KENTUCKY STATE LIBRARY JOURNAL

Department of Libraries
Box 537
Frankfort, Kentucky 40601

Subscription: Free to Kentucky libraries
Circulation: 1,800 (controlled)
Frequency: Irregular

Editor: Mike Averdick

Indexed in: Not specified

Description: This is a departmental newsletter for the exchange of
               service ideas. Articles pertain to the use of library services.

Contributors: Generally from within the state

Style requirements: Not specified

Number of manuscript
copies to submit: One

Approximate length
of manuscript: No set policy

Abstract requirement: None

Evaluation time: No set policy

Payment: None

THE LARC REPORTS
(formerly *LARC Newsletter*)

365 Ravello Lane
Costa Mesa, California 92627

Subscription: $50.00; free to members of LARC Association
Circulation: Not specified
Frequency: Quarterly

Editor: Barbara Evans Markuson

Address: The LARC Association
P.O. Box 27235
Tempe, Arizona 85282

Indexed in: Library Literature

Description: Periodical of the LARC Association (Library Automation, Research, and Consulting Association). Each issue deals with a single aspect of library automation.

Contributors: Authorities in the field

Style requirements: Not specified

Number of manuscript
copies to submit: One

Approximate length
of manuscript: 100 pages

Abstract requirement: None

Evaluation time: One month

Payment: None

LAW LIBRARY JOURNAL

American Association of Law Libraries
53 West Jackson Boulevard, Suite 1201
Chicago, Illinois

Subscription: $10.00
Circulation: 1,250
Frequency: Quarterly

Editor: Connie E. Bolden

Address: Washington State Law Library
               Temple of Justice
               Olympia, Washington 98504

Indexed in: Index to Legal Periodicals, Library Literature, Library and
               Information Science Abstracts

Description: Publication of the American Association of Law Libraries.
               Contains articles on law libraries and legal research.

Contributors: Primarily librarians

Style requirements: The journal has its own style manual.

Number of manuscript
copies to submit: Not specified

Approximate length
of manuscript: No set policy

Abstract requirement: None

Evaluation time: Seven to ten days

Payment: None

LEARNING TODAY: An Education Magazine of Library College Thought   (formerly *Library-College Journal*)

School of Library Science
University of Oklahoma
Box 956
Norman, Oklahoma 73096

Subscription: $10.00
Circulation: 2,000
Frequency: Quarterly

Editor: Howard Clayton

Indexed in: Library Literature

Description: Articles deal with the relationship between learning and libraries from kindergarten through graduate school, and with the teaching function of libraries.

Contributors: Primarily librarians. No author may contribute more than one manuscript per year.

Style requirements: Not specified

Number of manuscript
copies to submit: One

Approximate length
of manuscript: 1,800 to 2,500 words

Abstract requirement: None

Evaluation time: One month

Payment: None

LIBRARIANS' ADVOCATE
(supersedes *CU Voice*, which ceased publication in June 1970)

University Council–American Federation of Teachers
2510 Channing Way
Berkeley, California 94704

Subscription: $2.00
Circulation: 800
Frequency: Quarterly

Editor: Allan Covici

Indexed in: Not specified

Description: The *CU Voice* was limited to information about the Berkeley
              campus of the University of California, whereas the
              Librarians' Advocate is published for all nine campuses.
              This mimeographed publication pertains only to the
              University of California.

Contributors: No set policy

Style requirements: Not specified

Number of manuscript
copies to submit: One

Approximate length
of manuscript: Two to four pages

Abstract requirement: None

Evaluation time: One month

Payment: None

Additional
information: *Librarians' Advocate* began publication in
                      March 1972.

LIBRARY AND INFORMATION BULLETIN

The Library Association
7 Ridgmount Street
London, WC1E 7AE, England

Subscription: £1 per issue
Circulation: 700
Frequency: Three times per year

Editor: L. J. Taylor

Indexed in: Library and Information Science Abstracts

Description: This house journal contains articles relating to surveys and bibliographies. It is not open to outside contributors, except by occasional invitation of the editor.

Contributors: Primarily librarians

Style requirements: Not applicable

Number of manuscript
copies to submit: Not applicable

Approximate length
of manuscript: Not applicable

Abstract requirement: Not applicable

Evaluation time: Not applicable

Payment: None

LIBRARY ASSOCIATION OF ALBERTA. BULLETIN
(supersedes the *Alberta Library Association Bulletin*)

The Library Association of Alberta
Box 100
Lacombe, Alberta, Canada

Subscription: $10.00; free to members
Circulation: Not specified
Frequency: Quarterly

Editor: P. H. Connolly

Indexed in: Library Literature

Description: Contains articles of interest to Canadian librarians in all types of libraries. The journal also provides information about the activities of the Library Association of Alberta and about government publications.

Contributors: Members of the Library Association of Alberta and other librarians.

Style requirements: Not specified

Number of manuscript
copies to submit: Not specified

Approximate length
of manuscripts: Up to 2,000 words

Abstract requirement: None

Evaluation time: Not specified

Payment: None

LIBRARY ASSOCIATION RECORD

The Library Association
7 Ridgmount Street
London WC1E 7AE, England

Subscription: £8; free to members
Circulation: 19,500
Frequency: Monthly

Editor: Edward Dudley

Indexed in: Library Literature, Library and Information Science Abstracts, Current Index to Journals in Education

Description: This is the official journal of the British Library Association. Articles cover every phase of librarianship and are not limited to topics of interest to British librarians.

Contributors: Primarily librarians

Style requirements: Not specified

Number of manuscript
copies to submit: One

Approximate length
of manuscript: Up to 3,000 words

Abstract requirement: None

Evaluation time: Up to eight weeks

Payment: Not specified

LIBRARY CHRONICLE

University of Texas at Austin
P.O. Box 7219
Austin, Texas 78712

Subscription: $10.00
Circulation: 1,000
Frequency: Three times per year

Editor: Warren Roberts

Indexed in: Readers' Guide to Periodical Literature, MLA Abstracts, MLA International Bibliography

Description: "Articles devoted mainly to collections or aspects of collections at the Humanities Research Center; occasional articles of bibliographical interest not necessarily based on material at Austin. Subjects range from book illustrations, checklists of smaller manuscript and letter holdings, theatre materials, and photographic collections to literary portraits, typographical material, authors' libraries, and essays on manuscript collections of specific authors."

Contributors: Scholars and graduate students

Style requirements: *MLA Style Sheet* or *A Manual of Style* (University of Chicago Press)

Number of manuscript
copies to submit: One

Approximate length
of manuscripts: 2,000 to 6,500 words

Abstract requirement: Abstract due upon acceptance for publication.

Evaluation time: Four weeks

Payment: None

THE LIBRARY CHRONICLE

Van Pel Library
University of Pennsylvania
Philadelphia, Pennsylvania 19174

Subscription: $6.00; free to members of the Friends of the Library
Circulation: 750
Frequency: Semi-annual

Editor: William E. Miller

Indexed in: MLA Abstracts, MLA International Bibliography

Description: Published by the Friends of the Library. Preference is given to articles and notes on the possessions of the University of Pennsylvania Libraries. Not restricted to bibliographies or to library-oriented articles, but most articles deal with library holdings.

Contributors: Generally scholars, not necessarily from the University of Pennsylvania. Many contributors are specialists in language and literature.

Style requirements: Modified *MLA Style Sheet*

Number of manuscript
copies to submit: Two

Approximate length
of manuscript: No set policy; longer articles may be divided between two issues.

Abstract requirement: MLA Abstracts will send the author a form.

Evaluation time: Generally up to six weeks; longer if outside evaluation is required

Payment: 25 free offprints

Additional
information: Distributed to most of the major libraries in the world on an international exchange program.

LIBRARY HISTORY

The Library Association
7 Ridgmount Street
London WC1 7AE, England

Subscription: $3.50; free to members
Circulation: 1,600
Frequency: Semi-annual

Editor: P. A. Hoare

Address: Brynmor Jones Library
               The University
               Hull HU6 7RX, England

Indexed in: British Humanities Index, Historical Abstracts, Library
               Literature, Library and Information Science Abstracts

Description: Scholarly articles on the history of British and European
               libraries. Articles are based on research using unpublished
               source materal.

Contributors: Librarians and library school faculty

Style requirements: Not specified

Number of manuscript
copies to submit: One

Approximate length
of manuscript: Not over 7,000 words except by special agreement

Abstract requirement: None

Evaluation time: One week to two months

Payment: None

Additional
information: A preliminary inquiry about publication is
                       encouraged.

LIBRARY JOURNAL

1180 Avenue of the Americas
New York, New York 10036

Subscription: $15.00
Circulation: 36,000
Frequency: Semi-monthly, September to June; monthly in July and August

Editor: John N. Berry, III

Indexed in: Book Review Digest, Library Literature, Library Science
Abstracts, Readers' Guide to Periodical Literature, Book
Review Index, PAIS

Description: The aim of the journal is "to provide news, information,
thought, debate, in all areas of librarianship and library
service; to provide the most extensive reviewing services
possible to assist librarians in the selection of books, records,
and others materials." Most articles deal with practical
aspects of library activities or with new events of general
interest to librarianship. Contemporary social and political
problems of libraries (such as censorship) receive more emphasis here than in other library publications.

Contributors: Librarians and others interested in the profession

Style requirements: Not specified

Number of manuscript
copies to submit: One

Approximate length
of manuscript: 2,000 to 3,000 words

Abstract requirement: None

Evaluation time: Four to eight weeks; ten weeks for seasonal or
special material

Payment: $50 to $250; $25 for news items

Additional
information: Authors' photographs often accompany articles.

LIBRARY NEWS BULLETIN

Washington State Library
Olympia, Washington 98504

Subscription: Free; interested individuals and libraries may ask to be put on the mailing list

Circulation: 3,000

Frequency: Quarterly

Editor: Charles A. Symon

Indexed in: Library Literature

Description: Most articles concern public library activities in the state of Washington. All articles pertain to the Pacific Northwest.

Contributors: Washington librarians and editorial researchers of the Washington State Library. Out-of-state contributions seldom used.

Style requirements: Clear, understandable English; otherwise not specified

Number of manuscript copies to submit: One

Approximate length of manuscript: 500 to 1,200 words

Abstract requirement: None

Evaluation time: Two weeks

Payment: Complimentary copies only

Additional information: Articles often present workable and unworkable ideas accumulated from various libraries' attempts at innovation.

LIBRARY NOTES

Perkins Library
Duke University
Durham, North Carolina 27706

Subscription: $10.00
Circulation: 1,200
Frequency: Semi-annual

Editor: Not specified

Indexed in: Not specified

Description: Bibliographical and manuscript studies relating to the Medieval, Renaissance, and Byzantine periods.

Contributors: Primarily librarians

Style requirements: *A Manual of Style* (University of Chicago Press)

Number of manuscript
copies to submit: One

Approximate length
of manuscript: 2,000 to 3,000 words

Abstract requirement: None

Evaluation time: Up to six weeks

Payment: None

LIBRARY NOTES

Washington University School of Medicine
Medical Library
4580 Scott Avenue
St. Louis, Missouri 63110

Subscription: $1.00; $2.00 foreign
Circulation: Not specified
Frequency: Eight times per year

Editor: Staff of Medical Library, Washington University

Indexed in: Not specified

Description: Articles relate to medicine and libraries.

Contributors: Primarily librarians

Style requirements: Not specified

Number of manuscript
copies to submit: One

Approximate length
of manuscript: No set policy

Abstract requirement: None

Evaluation time: No set policy

Payment: Yes

LIBRARY OCCURRENT

Indiana State Library
140 North Senate Avenue
Indianapolis, Indiana 46204

Subscription: Free to Indiana libraries
Circulation: 4,000
Frequency: Quarterly

Editor: Mrs. M. J. Smith

Indexed in: Library Literature

Description: Contains articles on libraries, particularly those in Indiana.

Contributors: Librarians and trustees

Style requirements: Not specified

Number of manuscript
copies to submit: Two

Approximate length
of manuscript: 1,500 to 2,000 words

Abstract requirement: None

Evaluation time: Two weeks

Payment: None

THE LIBRARY QUARTERLY: A Journal of Investigation and Discussion in the Field of Library Science

Graduate Library School
University of Chicago
1100 East 57th Street
Chicago, Illinois 60637

Subscription: $10.00
Circulation: Approximately 3,700
Frequency: Quarterly

Editor: Lester Asheim

Indexed in: Library Literature, Book Review Digest, Book Review Index, Library and Information Science Abstracts, Current Index to Journals in Education, Historical Abstracts, America: History and Life, Information Science Abstracts

Description: A journal of research and investigation in the fields of library science and library education, with emphasis on historical, contemporary, rhetorical, and biographical problems. Reviews of library literature.

Contributors: Primarily librarians, but there are no restrictions.

Style requirements: *A Manual of Style* (University of Chicago Press); the journal will furnish style notes on request.

Number of manuscript
copies to submit: Two

Approximate length
of manuscript: 15 to 60 pages

Abstract requirement: Required (100 to 250 words)

Evaluation time: Four to six weeks

Payment: None, but authors receive 50 free copies of the published article.

LIBRARY RESOURCES AND TECHNICAL SERVICES

American Library Association
Resources and Technical Services Division
50 East Huron Street
Chicago, Illinois 60611

Subscription: $8.00; free to members of the Division
Circulation: 12,000
Frequency: Quarterly

Editor: Robert Wedgeworth

Indexed in: Library Literature, Library and Information Science Abstracts, Current Index to Journals in Education, Science Citation Index, Book Review Index, Book Review Digest

Description: Publication of the Resources and Technical Services Division of the American Library Association. Contains articles on technical services, library acquisitions, cataloging, classification, serials, and preservation of library materials.

Contributors: Primarily librarians

Style requirements: *A Manual of Style* (University of Chicago Press)

Number of manuscript
copies to submit: Two

Approximate length
of manuscript: 3,750 words

Abstract requirement: Required (75 to 100 words)

Evaluation time: Up to three months

Payment: None

Additional
information: Rejected manuscripts are criticized; if they are within the scope of the journal, they might be published after revisions. The Winter 1973 issue carried an announcement that Dr. Wesley Simonton, Professor of Library Science at the University of Minnesota, has recently been appointed editor.

LIBRARY SCIENCE WITH A SLANT TO DOCUMENTATION

c/o Documentation Research and Training Centre
112, Cross Road 11
Malleswaram, Bangalore 560003
India

Subscription: $10.00
Circulation: 400
Frequency: Quarterly

Editor: A. Neelameghan

Indexed in: Library and Information Science Abstracts, Information
              Science Abstracts, Library Literature

Description: Publishes original papers and scholarly review articles in
              the area of library science, including documentation.

Contributors: Librarians and information scientists from all over the world

Style requirements: Available on request

Number of manuscript
copies to submit: One

Approximate length
of mansucripts: No set policy

Abstract requirement: Yes

Evaluation time: Approximately two months

Payment: Reprints supplied to authors

THE LIBRARY: Transactions of the Bibliographical Society

Department of English
University of Birmingham
Birmingham, B15 2TT, England

Subscription: $6.70
Circulation: 1,250
Frequency: Quarterly

Editor: Peter Davison

Indexed in: Library Literature, Library and Information Science Abstracts

Description: Carries articles on the history of publishing and printing, rather than on librarianship. Topics are not restricted to events in Great Britain.

Contributors: Primarily people in the publishing field instead of librarians.

Style requirements: *MLA Style Sheet*; other information on request

Number of manuscript
copies to submit: One

Approximate length
of manuscript: No set policy

Abstract requirement: None

Evaluation time: Up to one month

Payment: None

Additional
information: Bibliographies and checklists are occasionally published. Most articles are in English.

LIBRARY TRENDS

Publications Office
Graduate School of Library Science
University of Illinois
Urbana, Illinois 61801

Subscription: $8.00
Circulation: 4,300
Frequency: Quarterly

Editor: Herbert Goldhor

Address: Publications Office, Library Trends
215 Armory Building
University of Illinois Graduate School of Library Science
Champaign, Illinois 61820

Indexed in: Library Literature, PAIS, Library and Information Science Abstracts, Current Contents, Current Index to Journals in Education, Science Citation Index

Description: Each issue deals with a specific predetermined topic of librarianship. The journal evaluates current thought and practices, and is concerned with conditions and movements rather than with describing individual institutions or practices.

Contributors: All articles are assigned by the issue editor, usually to librarians considered to be authorities on the subject.

Style requirements: Not applicable

Number of manuscript
copies to submit: Not applicable

Approximate length
of manuscript: Not applicable

Abstract requirement: Not applicable

Evaluation time: Not applicable

Payment: Not applicable

Additional
information: Because manuscripts are specifically solicited by the issue editor, policy requirements are explained once the contributor has agreed to cooperate in the project. Topics are usually assigned a year in advance.

LIBRI: International Library Review and IFLA Communications

Danmarks Biblioteksskole	(for editorial correspondence
Berketinget 6, DK-2300	and for submitting manuscripts
Copenhagen S, Denmark	for publication)

P. Harvard-Villisms	(for manuscripts and correspondence
Professor of Library Science	regarding IFLA communications)
Loughborough University of Technology	
Loughborough, England	

Subscription: $23.60
Circulation: 1,100
Frequency: Quarterly

Editor: Palle Birkelund, Preben Kirkegaard, Torkil Olsen

Indexed in: PAIS, Library Literature, Library and Information Science Abstracts

Description: Publishes articles on all phases of library science, including the history of books and publishing.

Contributors: Primarily librarians

Style requirements: Style notes are on the inside back cover of the periodical or will be furnished on request by the editor. Footnotes should be at the end of the paper; *ibid.* and *op. cit.* should be avoided.

Number of manuscript
copies to submit: One

Approximate length
of manuscript: 1,500 to 3,000 words

Abstract requirement: None

Evaluation time: One to three months

Payment: 20 Danish kroner per page, and 50 free copies of the article

Additional
information: Articles may be in English, French, or German.

MLA NEWSLETTER
(supersedes *M.L.A. Quarterly*)

10 South Seventh Street
Columbia, Missouri 65201

Subscription: $3.00; free to members of the Missouri Library Association
Circulation: 2,000
Frequency: Six times per year

Editor: Nancy Doyle

Indexed in: Not specified

Description: Official publication of the Missouri Library Association.
             Articles pertain to libraries and librarianship.

Contributors: Primarily librarians

Style requirements: Not specified

Number of manuscript
copies to submit: One

Approximate length
of manuscript: Up to 1,500 words

Abstract requirement: None

Evaluation time: Up to four weeks

Payment: None

MANUSCRIPTS

1023 Amherst
Tyler, Texas 75701

Subscription: $10.00; free to members of the Manuscript Society
Circulation: Approximately 1,100
Frequency: Quarterly

Editor: Paul V. Lutz

Indexed in: Not specified

Description: Articles discuss the collection, use, and preservation of
              primary manuscript material.

Contributors: Librarians and scholars concerned with manuscript material.

Style requirements: *A Manual of Style* (University of Chicago Press)

Number of manuscript
copies to submit: Two

Approximate length
of manuscript: Up to 3,000 words

Abstract requirement: None

Evaluation time: Two to three weeks

Payment: None; five free copies furnished

MEDIA: Library Services Journal

The Sunday School Board of the Southern Baptist Convention
127 Ninth Avenue, North
Nashville, Tennessee 37324

Subscription: $2.50
Circulation: 16,500
Frequency: Quarterly

Editor: Wayne E. Todd

Indexed in: Southern Baptist Periodical Index. The July-September issue
               of *Media* contains an index of the previous year's articles.

Description: Carries articles related to media, church library services, and
               audiovisuals. Material should be practical for church library
               staffs and should appeal to adults and church leaders in all
               denominations. Includes how-to articles as well as personal
               experience and inspirational items. Each item in *Media* is
               assigned a subject heading and a class number by a pro-
               fessional librarian on the staff.

Contributors: Library staff members in churches or interested individuals
               who have observed church library services.

Style requirements: *A Manual of Style* (University of Chicago Press)

Number of manuscript
copies to submit: One

Approximate length
of manuscript: 1,000 words, typed 35 or 55 characters per line,
                       25 lines per page. Human interest material and
                       "attention getters" are of varying lengths.

Abstract requirement: None

Evaluation time: One month

Payment: $0.025 per word; occasionally as much as $0.03 per
                      word. Publisher purchases all rights.

MICHIGAN LIBRARIAN

Michigan Library Association
226 West Washtenaw
Lansing, Michigan 48933

Subscription: $4.00; free to members
Circulation: 1,725
Frequency: Quarterly

Editor: Mrs. J. F. Pletz

Indexed in: Library Literature

Description: Official publication of the Michigan Library Association.
              Most articles are of interest to Michigan libraries. Each issue
              provides three to five articles, on a given theme; one of these
              articles will usually be of interest to librarians outside the
              state. The editorial staff hopes to attract more articles of
              interest outside the state.

Contributors: Primarily Michigan librarians, but others are invited to
              submit manuscripts.

Style requirements: Not specified

Number of manuscript
copies to submit: One

Approximate length
of manuscript: Four to sixteen typed pages

Abstract requirement: None

Evaluation time: Up to four weeks

Payment: None

Additional
information: An inquiry should precede submission of a
                         manuscript.

MICROFORM REVIEW

Rogues Ridge
Weston, Connecticut 06880

Subscription: $20.00
Circulation: 1,300
Frequency: Quarterly

Editor: Allen B. Veaner

Address: P.O. Box 9015
              Stanford, California 94305

Indexed in: Library Literature, Information Science Abstracts, Library
              and Information Science Abstracts

Description: Reviews micropublications for libraries, with some articles
              on using microforms in the library.

Contributors: Librarians and faculty members

Style requirements: Reviews and articles should be typed double-spaced
                      on 8½ by 11" paper, with the author's name at the
                      top of each page. Footnotes come at the end of the
                      article.

Number of manuscript
copies to submit: Two

Approximate length
of manuscripts: Reviews, 500 to 2,000 words; articles, 5,000 words

Abstract requirement: Required (75 to 100 words)

Evaluation time: Two months

Payment: None. However, reviewers receive 10 copies of the
                      review, one copy of the journal, and the choice of
                      one book for a list of about 50 reference titles.
                      Authors of articles receive two copies of the issue
                      and 10 copies of their article.

Additional
information: Authors should include a biographical note con-
                      sisting of present position and any other pertinent
                      information of interest to the reader.

MINNESOTA LIBRARIES

Minnesota State Department of Education
Library Division
117 University Avenue
St. Paul, Minnesota 55101

Subscription: Free to Minnesota libraries; exchange basis for other libraries
Circulation: 2,000
Frequency: Quarterly

Editor: Hannis S. Smith

Indexed in: Library Literature, Library and Information Science Abstracts

Description: Carries articles on Minnesota libraries and librarianship in
general. The scope is broad but excludes library service
developments, philosophy, and technological applications.
It is not limited to articles on librarianship within the
state or on research materials at the state university.

Contributors: Librarians, trustees, students, researchers. Usually an author
is limited to one article per year.

Style requirements: Not specified

Number of manuscript
copies to submit: Two

Approximate length
of manuscript: 4 to 24 pages, but generally 8 to 12 pages

Abstract requirement: None

Evaluation time: Up to two months

Payment: None

MISSISSIPPI LIBRARY NEWS

P.O. Box 127
Clinton, Mississippi 39056

Subscription: $5.00; free to members of the Mississippi Library Association
Circulation: 1,500
Frequency: Quarterly

Editor: J. B. Howell

Indexed in: Library Literature

Description: Contains articles of interest to Mississippi librarians.

Contributors: Primarily librarians

Style requirements: Typewritten, double-spaced, 8½ by 11" paper; other requirements not specified

Number of manuscript
copies to submit: One

Approximate length
of manuscript: Up to 1,000 words

Abstract requirement: None

Evaluation time: Up to four weeks; manuscripts should be submitted by the eighth of the month prior to publication.

Payment: None, but the author receives marked copies on publication.

MOUNTAIN PLAINS LIBRARY QUARTERLY

106 South 55th Street
Omaha, Nebraska 68132

Subscription: $2.00; free to members of Mountain Plains Library Assn.
Circulation: 1,000
Frequency: Quarterly

Editor: John M. Christ

Indexed in: Library Literature

Description: Publication of the Mountain Plains Library Association
             (Colorado, Kansas, Nebraska, Nevada, North Dakota, South
             Dakota, Utah, and Wyoming). Provides Association news
             and both technical and general articles on the subject of
             libraries as social institutions. At attempt is also made to
             acquaint non-librarians with the complexities of librarian-
             ship. Other features include poetry, short stories, cartoons,
             and crossword puzzles that are related to libraries and
             library services.

Contributors: Primarily librarians

Style requirements: Not specified

Number of manuscript
copies to submit: One

Approximate length
of manuscript: Up to 3,500 words (longer material will be
                       serialized)

Abstract requirement: None

Evaluation time: Three weeks

Payment: None

MOUSAION

University of South Africa
181 East Avenue
Pretoria, South Africa

Subscription: 5s. per issue, or on an exchange basis
Circulation: Approximately 400
Frequency: Six to eight times per year

Editor: H. J. deVleeschauwer

Indexed in: Library Literature, Library and Information Science Abstracts

Description: Similar to the University of Illinois Occasional Papers; covers all aspects of librarianship. Texts are in English, French, and German.

Contributors: Primarily librarians

Style requirements: Not specified

Number of manuscript
copies to submit: One

Approximate length
of manuscript: No set policy

Abstract requirement: None

Evaluation time: Up to ten weeks

Payment: Not specified

NEBRASKA LIBRARY ASSOCIATION QUARTERLY

(supersedes *Nebraska Library Association Newsletter*)

615 Lincoln Building
Lincoln, Nebraska 68508

Subscription: $5.00; free to members
Circulation: 900
Frequency: Quarterly

Editor: Louis B. Shelledy
Address: 3420 South 37th Street
            Lincoln, Nebraska 68508

Indexed in: Not specified

Description: Carries articles of interest to Nebraska librarians.

Contributors: Primarily librarians

Style requirements: Not specified

Number of manuscript
copies to submit: One

Approximate length
of manuscript: Up to 1,500 words

Abstract requirement: None

Evaluation time: Not specified

Payment: None

NEVADA LIBRARiES

Field Services Division
Nevada State Library
Carson City, Nevada 89701

Subscription: $2.00; free to members of the Nevada Library Association
Circulation: 520
Frequency: Five times per year

Editor: Barbara J. Mauseth

Indexed in: Not specified

Description: Published jointly by the Nevada Library Association and the Nevada State Library. It disseminates news of the association and the state library throughout the state, with the aim of reaching not only librarians but also state legislators.

Contributors: Association members, library agency staff, and members of the Nevada Council on Libraries

Style requirements: State Printing Office Style Manual

Number of manuscript
copies to submit: Not specified

Approximate length
of manuscript: Not specified

Abstract requirement: Not specified

Evaluation time: Not specified

Payment: None

Additional
information: According to the editor, there is an "infrequent use of 'special' articles."

NEW LIBRARY WORLD

Clive Bingley (Journals), Ltd.
16 Pembridge Road
London W11, England

Subscription: £5; $14.00
Circulation: 1,500
Frequency: Monthly

Editor: Clive Bingley

Indexed in: Library and Information Science Abstracts

Description: Carries articles on various aspects of professional librarianship.

Contributors: Librarians

Style requirements: Not specified

Number of manuscript
copies to submit: One

Approximate length
of manuscript: 1,000 words

Abstract requirement: None

Evaluation time: Not specified

Payment: "Modest"

NEW ZEALAND LIBRARIES

New Zealand Library Association
10 Park Street
Wellington 1, New Zealand

Subscription: NZ$2.40; free to members
Circulation:　1,800
Frequency:　Bimonthly

Editor:　J. W. Blackwood

Address:　The Library
　　　　　Massey University
　　　　　Palmerston North
　　　　　New Zealand

Indexed in:　Library Literature, Library and Information Science
　　　　　Abstracts, Index to New Zealand Periodicals

Description:　As the journal of the New Zealand Library Association, it
　　　　　provides material of professional interest to librarians in New
　　　　　Zealand. It serves as a forum through which members of the
　　　　　Association may make available to others their opinions, views,
　　　　　or the results of their experience on matters of library interest.

Contributors:　Mostly practicing librarians in New Zealand

Style requirements:　New Zealand Government Printing Office. *Style Book*.
　　　　　Also, the *New Zealand Libraries Notes for Contributors* is available upon request.

Number of manuscript
copies to submit:　Two

Approximate length
of manuscript:　Prospective contributors are advised to communicate
　　　　　with the editor in advance, so that he can advise on
　　　　　the length of the article.

Abstract requirement:　Required (not more than 100 words)

Evaluation time:　Contributions are normally required two months in
　　　　　advance of publication date.

Payment:　10 offprints

Additional
information:　"It would be appreciated if contributors would
　　　　　indicate when submitting material whether or not
　　　　　they are prepared to allow the Editor a free hand in
　　　　　dealing with it."

NEWBERRY LIBRARY BULLETIN

The Newberry Library
60 West Walton Street
Chicago, Illinois 60610

Subscription: Free; back issues, $0.75 per issue
Circulation: Not specified
Frequency: Quarterly through 1966, but only one issue since then. It is currently quite irregular, but plans are being made to remedy this situation.

Editor: James M. Wells

Indexed in: MLA International Bibliography

Description: Contains articles on materials in the library or involving research done there.

Contributors: Newberry staff and researchers

Style requirements: *MLA Handbook; A Manual of Style* (University of Chicago Press)

Number of manuscript
copies to submit: One

Approximate length
of manuscript: 5,000 words

Abstract requirement: Not required, but helpful

Evaluation time: Two months

Payment: None

Additional
information: The bulletin is distributed to all interested libraries and individuals, foreign and domestic.

NEWSLETTER ON INTELLECTUAL FREEDOM

50 East Huron Street
Chicago, Illinois 60611

Subscription: $5.00
Circulation: 3,000
Frequency: Bimonthly

Editors: Judith F. Krug and James A. Harvey

Indexed in: Library Literature

Description: Contains articles on censorship, intellectual freedom in
              libraries, etc.

Contributors: Primarily librarians

Style requirements: *A Manual of Style* (University of Chicago Press)

Number of manuscript
copies to submit: One

Approximate length
of manuscript: 1,500 to 2,500 words

Abstract requirement: None

Evaluation time: Two weeks

Payment: Copies of issue

NORTH CAROLINA LIBRARIES

Box 212, ASU Station
Appalachian State University
Boone, North Carolina 28607

Subscription: $3.00; free to members of North Carolina Library Association
Circulation: 2,000
Frequency: Quarterly

Editor: Herbert Poole

Address: Guilford College
Greensboro, North Carolina 27410

Indexed in: Library Literature. The journal carries its own index in each biennial issue.

Description: Contains articles of interest to North Carolina libraries.

Contributors: Students, librarians, and teachers

Style requirements: Not specified

Number of manuscript
copies to submit: One

Approximate length
of manuscript: Up to 1,000 words

Abstract requirement: None

Evaluation time: Up to four weeks

Payment: None

OHIO LIBRARY ASSOCIATION BULLETIN (OLA Bulletin)

The Public Library of Youngstown and Mahoning County
Main Library
305 Wick Avenue
Youngstown, Ohio 44503

Subscription: Free to members
Circulation: Not specified
Frequency: Quarterly

Editor: Robert F. Cayton

Indexed in: Library Literature

Description: Contains articles on current issues, on libraries, or on Ohio.
               "Articles by the non-professional, the young librarian, the
               'older' librarian facing a new challenge, will be welcomed."

Contributors: Not specified

Style requirements: Illustrative material is encouraged. The use of foot-
                         notes is discouraged. Manuscripts should be typed
                         with 43 characters to a line. Editorial policy can
                         be found at the back of the January 1973 issue.

Number of manuscript
copies to submit: One

Approximate length
of manuscript: No set policy, but shorter articles are preferred.

Abstract requirement: None. "If one were sent, it would be printed
                         instead of the article."

Evaluation time: One week

Payment: None

OKLAHOMA LIBRARIAN

401 West Brooks
Norman, Oklahoma 73069

Subscription: $10.00; free to members of the Oklahoma Library Association
Circulation: 800
Frequency: Quarterly

Editor: James K. Zink

Indexed in: Library Literature

Description: As the official bulletin of the Oklahoma Library Association, it carries articles (informational, analytical, and research) pertaining to librarianship.

Contributors: Primarily librarians

Style requirements: *A Manual of Style* (University of Chicago Press)

Number of manuscript
copies to submit: One

Approximate length
of manuscript: No set policy

Abstract requirement: None

Evaluation time: One to six months

Payment: None

Additional
information: Manuscripts must be submitted at least six weeks in advance of expected publication date.

ONTARIO LIBRARY REVIEW

Provincial Library Service
14th Floor
Mowat Block, Queen's Park
Toronto 182, Ontario, Canada

Subscription: $3.00 for three years
Circulation: 6,300
Frequency: Quarterly

Editor: Irma McDonough

Indexed in: Library Literature, Library and Information Science
               Abstracts, Canadian Periodical Index

Description: There are articles on librarianship in general as well as specific
               reports relating to Ontario libraries. The general articles
               cover a wide range of topics and will be of interest to school,
               public, and academic libraries.

Contributors: Primarily librarians

Style requirements: Not specified

Number of manuscript
copies to submit: One

Approximate length
of manuscript: Up to 2,500 words

Abstract requirement: None

Evaluation time: Not specified

Payment: None

PACIFIC NORTHWEST LIBRARY ASSOCIATION QUARTERLY
(PNLA Quarterly)

Southern Oregon College
Ashland, Oregon 97520

Subscription: $5.00; free to members
Circulation: 1,500
Frequency: Quarterly

Editor: Richard E. Moore

Indexed in: Current Contents, Library Literature, Library and Information
              Science Abstracts

Description: Official organ of the Pacific Northwest Library Association.
              Emphasizes the Pacific Northwest (Alaska, British Columbia,
              Idaho, Montana, Oregon, and Washington).

Contributors: Primarily librarians

Style requirements: *A Manual of Style* (University of Chicago Press)

Number of manuscript
copies to submit: One

Approximate length
of manuscript: 3,500 words

Abstract requirement: None

Evaluation time: Six weeks

Payment: None

PENNSYLVANIA LIBRARY ASSOCIATION BULLETIN

Room 506
2006 Craig Street
Pittsburgh, Pennsylvania 15213

Subscription:	$5.00; free to members
Circulation:	3,700
Frequency:	Bimonthly

Editor: Elinore S. Thomas

Address: Graduate School of Library and Information Science
University of Pittsburgh
Pittsburgh, Pennsylvania 15213

Indexed in: Library Literature, Library and Information Science Abstracts

Description: Carries articles pertaining to librarianship; not limited to
articles of interest to Pennsylvania librarians.

Contributors: Primarily librarians

Style requirements: Typewritten, double-spaced; no style manual
specified

Number of manuscript
copies to submit: One

Approximate length
of manuscript: No set policy

Abstract requirement: None

Payment: None

Additional
information: Manuscripts should be submitted at least six weeks
before scheduled date of publication.

PRINCETON UNIVERSITY LIBRARY CHRONICLE

Princeton University Library
Friends of the Library
Princeton, New Jersey 08540

Subscription: $7.50; single issue, $2.50
Circulation: 2,000
Frequency: Three times per year

Editor: Mina R. Bryan

Indexed in: Not specified; however, the publication has an index for
              volumes 1 through 25 (1939-1964), which costs $10.00.

Description: Publication of the Friends of the Princeton University Library.
             It draws on the special collections of the University and the
             resources of the Department of Rare Books.

Contributors: Members of the Princeton faculty and researchers at the
              Princeton library.

Style requirements: *MLA Style Manual*

Number of manuscript
copies to submit: One

Approximate length
of manuscript: 15 to 20 pages

Abstract requirement: None

Evaluation time: Two weeks

Payment: None

Additional
information: Neither advertising nor book reviews are accepted.

PUBLISHER'S WEEKLY: The Book Industry Journal

R. R. Bowker and Company
1180 Avenue of the Americas
New York, New York 10036

Subscription: $18.50
Circulation: 28,000
Frequency: Weekly

Editor: Arnold W. Ehrlich

Indexed in: Business Periodicals Index, Library Literature, Readers'
                Guide to Periodical Literature, Chemical Abstracts

Description: Carries articles of interest to librarians and the book trade,
                dealing with such topics as publishing, libraries, and book
                selling.

Contributors: Primarily librarians and members of the book trade

Style requirements: Not specified

Number of manuscript
copies to submit: One

Approximate length
of manuscripts: Not specified

Abstract requirement: Required

Evaluation time: One week

Payment: $50.00 per printed page

RQ

Reference and Adult Services Division of the American Library Association
1201-05 Bluff Street
Fulton, Missouri 65251

Subscription: $5.00; free to members of the Division
Circulation: 7,005
Frequency: Quarterly

Editor: William A. Katz

Address: School of Library and Information Science
State University of New York at Albany
1223 Western Avenue
Albany, New York 12203

Indexed in: Library Literature, Library and Information Science Abstracts

Description: Official journal of the Reference and Adult Services Division of the American Library Association. Articles cover reference services and bibliography for school, public, and academic libraries. There are regular columns on government documents, reference research, difficult reference questions, and short book reviews of reference titles.

Contributors: Theorists and those interested in working in reference service. Only one manuscript is accepted per year from a contributor.

Style requirements: Not specified

Number of manuscript
copies to submit: One

Approximate length
of manuscripts: No set policy

Abstract requirement: None

Evaluation time: Two to four weeks

Payment: Two free copies of the issue

Additional
information: Beginning with the Fall 1973 issue, all manuscripts should be sent to the new editor: Dennis Ribbens, Director, Lawrence University Library, Appleton, Wisconsin 54911.

RESEARCH IN LIBRARIANSHIP

34 Norfolk Street
Werneth, Oldham
(Lancs.) England

Subscription: $4.25
Circulation: 600
Frequency: Three issues per year

Editor: Edward R. Reid-Smith

Indexed in: Library and Information Science Abstracts

Description: "Articles on research methods; reports of projects completed; news-items on current work; book reviews; abstracts of theses. Coverage of articles largely British but overseas articles welcomed; news-items chiefly British and American; theses British; reviews international. As overseas subscriptions increase, so world-wide coverage of contents has increased."

Contributors: Librarians and authorities on specific topics

Style requirements: "Largely left to contributors, as we do not aim to be restrictive; clarity of expression is essential because of the large number of overseas subscribers."

Number of manuscript
copies to submit: One

Approximate length
of manuscript: No set policy; longer manuscripts are serialized

Abstract requirement: Required

Evaluation time: Generally two to three weeks, unless extensive comments or suggestions are made

Payment: None

Additional
informaiton: Some lengthy manuscripts are printed in pamphlet form. *Research in Librarianship* is a non-profit venture.

SLA GEOGRAPHY AND MAP DIVISION BULLETIN

American Geographical Society Library
Broadway at 156th Street
New York, New York 10032

Subscription: $7.50
Circulation: Approximately 850
Frequency: Quarterly

Editor: Lynn S. Mullins

Indexed in: Information Science Abstracts, Library and Information Science Abstracts, Library Literature

Description: Primarily publishes research articles and news items in the field of geographic and cartographic bibliography, literature, libraries, and collections. Original articles are carried on research problems, mapping programs, classification systems, historical studies, subject bibliographies, descriptions of collections, etc. In addition, the journal provides new book and map lists and serves as a forum for the exchange of recent news, ideas, and techniques in the handling of these materials.

Contributors: "Open to anyone"

Style requirements: Manuscripts should be typed, double-spaced.

Number of manuscript copies to submit: One

Approximate length of manuscript: Up to 25 pages

Abstract requirement: None

Evaluation time: Two weeks

Payment: Free copies of issue

THE SCHOOL LIBRARIAN: The Journal of the School Library Association (formerly *School Librarian and School Library Review*)

Premier House
150 Southampton Row
London WC1B 5AR, England

Subscription: £4.50; free to members
Circulation: 7,000
Frequency: Quarterly

Editor: Norman Furlong
Address: 5 Shore Close
Silverdale, Carnforth
Lancs, England

Indexed in: British Education Index, Library Literature, Library and Information Science Abstracts

Description: Official bulletin of the School Library Association, London. Carries articles that relate school libraries to the educational process and that describe practical experiences.

Contributors: Primarily teachers and librarians in Great Britain.

Style requirements: The periodical itself should be consulted as a style guide for footnotes and bibliography.

Number of manuscript
copies to submit: One

Approximate length
of manuscripts: 1,500 to 2,000 words

Abstract requirement: None

Evaluation time: Up to eight weeks

Payment: None

SCHOOL LIBRARY JOURNAL: The Magazine for Children's, Young Adult, and School Librarians

1180 Avenue of the Americas
New York, New York 10036

Subscription: $10.00
Circulation: 27,000
Frequency: Monthly September-May, in the last issue of the month of *Library Journal*

Editor: Lillian N. Gerhardt

Indexed in: Library Literature, Library and Information Science Abstracts, Readers' Guide to Periodical Literature

Description: Carries articles on topics of interest to school librarians and others working with children. Articles often deal with controversial issues.

Contributors: Experts in the field

Style requirements: Not specified

Number of manuscript
copies to submit: One

Approximate length
of manuscript: 1,000 to 3,000 words

Abstract requirement: None

Evaluation time: Four to eight weeks

Payment: $50 to $250; $25 for news items

Additional
information: Author's photograph accompanies the article.

SCHOOL MEDIA QUARTERLY
(formerly *School Libraries*)

American Association of School Librarians
50 East Huron Street
Chicago, Illinois 60611

Subscription: $6.00; free to members of the Association
Circulation: 15,000
Frequency: Quarterly

Editor: Glenn E. Estes
Address: 804 Volunteer Boulevard
               Knoxville, Tennessee 37916

Indexed in: Book Review Index, Current Contents, Library Literature,
               Current Index to Journals in Education

Description: Official publication of American Association of School
               Librarians, a division of the American Library Association
               and an associated organization of the National Education
               Association. Carries articles that deal with school library
               media services and library media use.

Contributors: School librarians, media specialists, and faculty

Style requirements: *A Manual of Style* (Univeristy of Chicago Press)

Number of manuscript
copies to submit: Two

Approximate length
of manuscripts: No set policy

Abstract requirement: None

Evaluation time: Not specified

Payment: None

Additional
information: Rejected manuscripts are returned to authors only
                       upon request.

THE SERIF

Kent State University Libraries
Kent, Ohio 44242

Subscription: $6.00
Circulation: Approximately 275
Frequency: Quarterly

Editor: Dean H. Keller

Indexed in: Not specified

Description: Carries articles on bibliography, book collecting, and rare
               books.

Contributors: Primarily librarians

Style requirements: *MLA Style Sheet*

Number of manuscript
copies to submit: One

Approximate length
of manuscript: No set policy

Abstract requirement: None

Evaluation time: One to two months

Payment: Five free copies of the issue in which the
                         article appears

SOUTH DAKOTA LIBRARY BULLETIN

South Dakota State Library Commission
Pierre, South Dakota 57501

Subscription: Free to South Dakota libraries
Circulation: 1,500
Frequency: Quarterly

Editor: Mercedes B. MacKay

Indexed in: Library Literature

Description: Carries articles of interest to South Dakota librarians and
               articles related to the improvement of public library service.

Contributors: Primarily librarians

Style requirements: Not specified

Number of manuscript
copies to submit: One

Approximate length
of manuscript: No set policy

Abstract requirement: None

Evaluation time: No set policy

Payment: None

SOUTHEASTERN LIBRARIAN

Box 1032
Decatur, Georgia 30030

Subscription: $6.00; free to members of the Southeastern Library Assn.
Circulation: Not specified
Frequency: Quarterly

Editor: Jerrold Orne and Ann W. Cobb

Indexed in: Library Literature, Library and Information Science Abstracts

Description: Publication of the Southeastern Library Association (Alabama, Georgia, Florida, Kentucky, Mississippi, North Carolina, South Carolina, Tennessee, and Virginia). Articles are of interest to libraries and librarianship outside the area as well as to those in the Southeast.

Contributors: Primarily librarians

Style requirements: Not specified

Number of manuscript
copies to submit: One

Approximate length
of manuscript: No set policy

Abstract requirement: None

Evaluation time: Up to six weeks

Payment: None

SPECIAL LIBRARIES

Special Libraries Association
235 Park Avenue South
New York, New York 10003

Subscription: $22.50; free to members
Circulation: 9,700
Frequency: 10 issues per year (monthly, but bimonthly from May
through August)

Editor: Janet D. Bailey

Indexed in: Business Periodicals Index, Library Literature, Library and
Information Science Abstracts, PAIS, Information Science
Abstracts, Historical Abstracts, Management Index, Science
Citation Index

Description: Official publication of the Special Libraries Association.
Carries articles, reports, and book reviews of interest to the
special library profession.

Contributors: Librarians and specialists in the field

Style requirements: *A Manual of Style* (University of Chicago Press)

Number of manuscript
copies to submit: One original, three photocopies

Approximate length
of manuscript: 1,000 to 5,000 words

Abstract requirement: Required (100 words)

Evaluation time: At least six weeks

Payment: None

TENNESSEE LIBRARIAN

Tennessee Library Association
Joint University Libraries
Nashville, Tennessee 37203

Subscription: $4.00; free to members
Circulation: 1,600
Frequency: Quarterly

Editor: Paul Murphy

Indexed in: Library Literature

Description: Publishes articles of any type, on many subjects

Contributors: Not necessarily librarians

Style requirements: Manuscript should be typed on legal-size paper

Number of manuscript
copies to submit: One

Approximate length
of manuscript: No set policy

Abstract requirement: None

Evaluation time: Up to four weeks

Payment: None

Additional
information: Evaluation consists of three readings.

TEXAS A AND M UNIVERSITY LIBRARY NOTES

Texas A and M University
University Library
College Station, Texas 77843

Subscription: Free
Circulation: Not specified
Frequency: Five times per year

Editor: Henry L. Alsmeyer, Jr.

Indexed in: Not specified

Description: Articles are primarily of interest to readers on the Texas
A and M University campus, since they pertain to materials
in the University libraries.

Contributors: Librarians and other faculty from the University

Style requirements: *MLA Style Sheet*

Number of manuscript
copies to submit: Not specified

Approximate length
of manuscript: No set policy

Abstract requirement: None

Evaluation time: Not specified

Payment: None

TEXAS LIBRARIES

Texas State Library
Texas Archives and Library Building
Box 12927
Capitol Station
Austin, Texas 78711

Subscription: Free to Texas libraries and American library schools
Circulation: 1,950
Frequency: Quarterly

Editor: Millicent Huff

Indexed in: Library Literature

Description: Includes articles of interest to Texas librarians and articles pertaining to the University of Texas

Contributors: Librarians and staff members

Style requirements: Not specified

Number of manuscript
copies to submit: One

Approximate length
of manuscript: Not specified

Abstract requirement: None

Evaluation time: Up to eight weeks

Payment: None

TEXAS LIBRARY JOURNAL

P.O. Box 7763, University Station
Austin, Texas 78712

Subscription: $2.00 single issue; free to members of Texas Library Assn.
Circulation: 3,200
Frequency: Five times per year

Editor: Mary Pound

Indexed in: Library Literature

Description: Publication of the Texas Library Association. Carries
               articles of interest to librarians in Texas and the Southwest.

Contributors: Primarily librarians

Style requirements: Not specified

Number of manuscript
copies to submit: Not specified

Approximate length
of manuscript: Four to five pages

Abstract requirement: None

Evaluation time: Up to two weeks

Payment: None

TOP OF THE NEWS

50 East Huron Street
Chicago, Illinois 60611

Subscription: $2.00; free to members of Children's Services Division
and Young Adult Services Division of ALA
Circulation: 15,000
Frequency: Quarterly

Editor: Mary Jane Anderson

Address: Baltimore County Public Library
Administrative Offices
25 West Chesapeake Avenue
Towson, Maryland 21204

Indexed in: Library Literature, Library and Information Science Abstracts,
Current Index to Journals in Education

Description: Published by the Children's Services Division and the Young
Adult Services Division of the American Library Association.
Carries articles relevant to elementary and high school
libraries, with book reviews and reviews of magazines for
young adults and for children.

Contributors: Librarians and educators

Style requirements: None

Number of manuscript
copies to submit: One

Approximate length
of manuscript: No set policy

Abstract requirement: None

Evaluation time: Four to six weeks

Payment: None

Additional
information: Articles are more popular than scholarly and give
practical advice.

UNESCO BULLETIN FOR LIBRARIES

UNESCO Bulletin for Libraries
Place de Fontenay
75 Paris 7e, France

Subscription: $4.00
Circulation: 1,600 in the United States
Frequency: Bimonthly

Editor: Mrs. I. Bettembourg

Indexed in: Library Literature, Library and Information Science
Abstracts, PAIS, Current Index to Journals in Education,
Computer and Control Abstracts, Current Contents

Description: An international journal on libraries, bibliographies, archives,
and documentation. Includes announcements of new library
publications and offers the exchange of publications.
Generally only invited papers are published, but exceptions
are made.

Contributors: Primarily librarians

Style requirements: Not specified

Number of manuscript
copies to submit: One

Approximate length
of manuscript: Not specified

Abstract requirement: Required

Evaluation time: Up to one month

Payment: None

Additional
information: Editions are in English, French, Russian, and
Spanish. If possible, illustrations should be included
with the manuscript.

UNIVERSITY OF ROCHESTER LIBRARY. BULLETIN.

University of Rochester Library
Rochester, New York 14627

Subscription: Free to Friends of the Library and to institutions
Circulation: 1,200
Frequency: Two or three issues per year

Editor: Robert L. Volz

Address: Rush Rhees Library
University of Rochester
River Station
Rochester, New York 14627

Indexed in: Not specified

Description: Articles deal with Rochester collections or with items in the University's collections.

Contributors: Faculty, library staff, and outside contributors

Style requirements: Not specified

Number of manuscript
copies to submit: One

Approximate length
of manuscript: Up to 75 pages; usual length is 4 to 12 pages

Abstract requirement: None

Evaluation time: No set policy

Payment: None

UTAH LIBRARIES

Utah State Library Commission
2150 South Second West
Salt Lake City, Utah 84115

Subscription: $2.00; free to members of the Utah Library Association
Circulation: 1,000
Frequency: Semiannual

Editor: Blaine H. Hall

Address: 505B JRC Library
Brigham Young University
Provo, Utah 84601

Indexed in: Library Literature

Description: Practical articles relating to Utah librarianship

Contributors: Not primarily librarians

Style requirements: *A Manual of Style* (University of Chicago Press)

Number of manuscript
copies to submit: One

Approximate length
of manuscript: 1,000 to 2,000 words

Abstract requirement: None

Evaluation time: Two weeks

Payment: None

Additional
information: Biographical information should be submitted
with the manuscript.

VERMONT LIBRARIES

State of Vermont
Department of Libraries
Montpelier, Vermon 05602

Subscription: Not specified
Circulation: Not specified
Frequency: Monthly, but bimonthly May through August

Editor: Henry Marcy

Indexed in: Library Literature

Description: Contains articles related to libraries and librarianship,
               particularly in Vermont.

Contributors: Primarily librarians

Style requirements: Not specified

Number of manuscript
copies to submit: One

Approximate length
of manuscript: One to six pages

Abstract requirement: None

Evaluation time: One to eight weeks

Payment: None

Additional
information: Photographs are published with articles.

VIRGINIA LIBRARIAN

5 Commander Drive
Hampton, Virginai 23366

Subscription: $3.00; free to members of the Virginia Library Association
Circulation: 1,300
Frequency: Quarterly plus annual proceedings issue

Editor: Dean Burgess

Address: Portsmouth Public Library
               601 Court Street
               Portsmouth, Virginia 23704

Indexed in: Library Literature

Description: Articles relating to Virginia libraries and librarians, usually
               of more appeal to a general library audience than to scholars.

Contributors: Primarily librarians

Style requirements: Not specified

Number of manuscript
copies to submit: One

Approximate length
of manuscript: Four to eight pages

Abstract requirement: None

Evaluation time: One to six months

Payment: None

Additional
information: The journal reserves the right to edit for length
                         without consulting the author.

WEST VIRGINIA LIBRARIES

West Virginia University Library
821 Price Street
Morgantown, West Virginia 26506

Subscription: $3.00; free to members of West Virginia Library Association
Circulation: 1,000
Frequency: Quarterly

Editor: Lois T. Murphy

Indexed in: Library Literature

Description: Articles deal with library and information sciences in West
             Virginia.

Contributors: Primarily librarians

Style requirements: Not specified

Number of manuscript
copies to submit: One

Approximate length
of manuscript: One to two pages

Abstract requirement: None

Evaluation time: One to three months

Payment: None

WILSON LIBRARY BULLETIN

950 University Avenue
Bronx, New York 10452

Subscription: $9.00
Circulation: 38,100
Frequency: Monthly, September to June

Editor: William R. Eshelman

Indexed in: Library Literature, Library and Information Science Abstracts, Readers' Guide to Periodical Literature, Book Review Index, America: History and Life, Education Index, Current Contents, Historical Abstracts

Description: Each issue is developed around a central theme. Articles deal with contemporary problems, news items, and trends of interest to librarianship.

Contributors: Primarily librarians, but also other experts on the topics under consideration

Style requirements: *A Manual of Style* (University of Chicago Press)

Number of manuscript copies to submit: Two

Approximate length of manuscript: 2,000 to 6,000 words

Abstract requirement: None

Evaluation time: Three to eight weeks

Payment: Between $10.00 and $150.00 per article

Additional information: Approximately 90 percent of the unsolicited manuscripts submitted are rejected; nevertheless, some 50 articles are published each year.

WISCONSIN LIBRARY BULLETIN

State Superintendent
Division for Library Services
Department of Public Instruction
126 Langdon Street
Madison, Wisconsin 53702

Subscription: $2.00; free to Wisconsin school and public libraries and to library boards
Circulation: 3,900
Frequency: Bimonthly

Editor: Beryl E. Hoyt

Indexed in: Library Literature

Description: Carries articles relating to libraries and media centers, their personnel, and their services.

Contributors: Primarily librarians, but also educators or people in a specific area related to library service. There is no policy limiting the number of manuscripts an author may publish per year.

Style requirements: Typed 75 characters per line; no other specifications

Number of manuscript
copies to submit: One

Approximate length
of manuscript: 400 to 2,000 words; generally 750 to 1,600 words

Abstract requirement: None

Evaluation: One to four weeks

Payment: None

Additional
information: Most articles are solicited, but there is a "Professional Voices" column that uses free-lance contributions.

YALE UNIVERSITY LIBRARY. GAZETTE

The Beinecke Rare Book and Manuscript Library
Yale University Library
Box 1603A Yale Station
New Haven, Connecticut 06520

Subscription: $6.00; single issue, $1.50
Circulation: Not specified
Frequency: Quarterly

Editor: Donald Gallup

Indexed in: Library Literature

Description: Publicizes the resources of the Yale University Library. Articles describe materials in the library or the use of these materials.

Contributors: Librarians and researchers

Style requirements: *MLA Style Sheet*

Number of manuscript
copies to submit: One

Approximate length
of manuscript: 1,000 words

Abstract requirement: None

Evaluation time: Not specified

Payment: None

ANNUALS, IRREGULAR SERIES,

MONOGRAPHIC SERIES

ADVANCES IN LIBRARIANSHIP

Academic Press, Inc.
111 Fifth Avenue
New York, New York 10003

Subscription: $14.00 to $16.00
Circulation: Not specified
Frequency: Annual

Editor: Melvin J. Voigt

Address: University of California
           San Diego Library
           La Jolla, California 92037

Indexed in: Library Literature

Description: Scholarly reviews of selected topics in librarianship. These
              critical articles are based on research and practice.

Contributors: By invitation of editor; primarily librarians and specialists
               in the field.

Style requirements: Not specified

Number of manuscript
copies to submit: Two

Approximate length
of manuscript: 30 to 70 pages

Abstract requirement: None

Evaluation time: No set policy

Payment: Royalties

C. C. WILLIAMSON MEMORIAL LECTURE

School of Library Science
George Peabody College for Teachers
Nashville, Tennessee 37203

Subscription: Free to selected mailing list; sent on request
Circulation: 500
Frequency: Annual

Editor: Edwin S. Gleaves

Indexed in: Library Literature

Description: This publication is based on a lecture given at the school; other manuscripts are not solicited.

Contributors: Invited speakers at the School of Library Science

Style requirements: Not applicable

Number of manuscript
copies to submit: Not applicable

Approximate length
of manuscript: Not applicable

Abstract requirement: Not applicable

Evaluation time: Not applicable

Payment: None

CANADIAN LIBRARY ASSOCIATION. OCCASIONAL PAPERS

Canadian Library Association
151 Sparks Street
Ottawa, Ontario K1P 5E3
Canada

Subscription: Varies
Circulation: 750
Frequency: Irregular

Editor: Louise Rickenbacker

Indexed in: Not specified

Description: Publishes manuscripts on libraries and librarianship

Contributors: Primarily librarians

Style requirements: Not specified

Number of manuscript
copies to submit: Not specified

Approximate length
of manuscript: No set policy; varies greatly

Abstract requirement: None

Evaluation time: Not specified

Payment: Not specified

COLUMBIA UNIVERSITY STUDIES IN LIBRARY SERVICE

Columbia University Press
562 West 113th Street
New York, New York 10025

Subscription: Varies
Circulation: Not specified
Frequency: Irregular

Editor: None

Indexed in: Library Literature

Description: A series of clothbound books on various topics in library science.

Contributors: Not specified

Style requirements: Varies with each book

Number of manuscript
copies to submit: Not specified

Approximate length
of manuscript: Not specified

Abstract requirement: None

Evaluation time: Not specified

Payment: Not specified

CONTRIBUTIONS IN LIBRARIANSHIP AND INFORMATION SCIENCE

Greenwood Press, Inc.
51 Riverside Avenue
Westport, Connecticut 06880

Subscription: Varies
Circulation: Not specified
Frequency: Irregular

Editor: Paul Wasserman

Address: University of Maryland
              College Park, Maryland 20742

Indexed in: Not specified

Description: The primary criterion for acceptance of a manuscript is
              whether the manuscript makes a genuine contribution to
              the knowledge base of the field of library or information
              science.

Contributors: Not specified

Style requirements: *A Manual of Style* (University of Chicago Press)

Number of manuscript
copies to submit: Two

Approximate length
of manuscript: No set policy

Abstract requirement: Outline of proposed subject required

Evaluation time: Six to eight weeks

Payment: Varies

DOUGLAS LIBRARY. OCCASIONAL PAPERS

Queen's University
Douglas Library
Kingston, Ontario, Canada

Subscription: Varies
Circulation: Not specified
Frequency: Irregular

Editor: Varies with each issue

Indexed in: Not specified

Description: Occasional monographic series on matters of interest to the Douglas Library.

Contributors: Library staff members

Style requirements: *A Manual of Style* (University of Chicago Press)

Number of manuscript
copies to submit: Not specified

Approximate length
of manuscript: Up to 5,000 words

Abstract requirement: None

Evaluation time: One month

Payment: None

Additional
information: Publication has been suspended until further notice.

GENESEO STUDIES IN LIBRARY AND INFORMATION SCIENCE

School of Library and Information Science
State University College of Arts and Science
Geneseo, New York 14454

Subscription: $4.50 (plus $0.18 postage)
Circulation: 300 to 600
Frequency: Irregular

Editor: Ivan L. Kaldor

Indexed in: Not specified

Description: "A forum for the publication of research papers, conference proceedings, text of memorial lectures, bibliographic studies, etc."

Contributors: "Any individual who has something to say about library and information science. Past contributors include Dr. Marshall McLuhan, Archibald MacLeish, Dr. John Kephart, Karl Shapiro and many others."

Style requirements: Not specified

Number of manuscript
copies to submit: Two

Approximate length
of manuscript: 120 to 150 pages

Abstract requirement: Required

Evaluation time: Six months

Payment: Modest honorarium based on sales

ILLINOIS STATE LIBRARY. MONOGRAPHIC WORK.

Publications Unit
Illinois State Library
Springfield, Illinois 62706

Subscription: Free
Circulation: 500
Frequency: Irregular

Editor: Irma Bostian

Indexed in: Not specified

Description: Surveys and studies conducted by the Illinois State Library

Contributors: Staff of the Illinois State Library

Style requirements: Not specified

Number of manuscript
copies to submit: Not applicable

Approximate length
of manuscript: Not applicable

Abstract requirement: Not applicable

Evaluation time: Not applicable

Payment: None

INTERNATIONAL SERIES OF MONOGRAPHS IN LIBRARY AND INFORMATION SCIENCES

Pergamon Press, Ltd.
Headington Hill Hall
Oxford, England

Subscription: Varies
Circulation: Approximately 3,000
Frequency: Irregular

Editor: G. Chandler

Indexed in: Not specified

Description: Volumes cover major aspects of librarianship and information science.

Contributors: Primarily librarians

Style requirements: Not specified

Number of manuscript
copies to submit: Not specified

Approximate length
of manuscript: Not specified

Abstract requirement: None

Evaluation time: Not specified

Payment: Not specified

Additional
information: Any additional information needed can be obtained through the editorial offices of the Pergamon Press.

LIBRARY SCIENCE TEXT SERIES

Libraries Unlimited, Inc.
P.O. Box 263
Littleton, Colorado 80120

Subscription: Varies; 10% discount on standing orders
Circulation: Varies
Frequency: One to three titles per year

Editor: Bohdan S. Wynar

Indexed in: Library Literature, Library and Information Science Abstracts

Description: The objective of this series is to provide the library profession
with clearly written and well-balanced texts for graduate and
undergraduate programs, as well as vocational education.

Contributors: Primarily librarians

Style requirements: *A Manual of Style* (University of Chicago Press)

Number of manuscript
copies to submit: One

Approximate length
of manuscript: 200 to 500 pages

Abstract requirement: None

Evaluation time: Four to six weeks

Payment: Royalties

METRO: NEW YORK METROPOLITAN REFERENCE AND RESEARCH LIBRARY AGENCY. METRO MISCELLANEOUS PUBLICATIONS SERIES

New York Metropolitan Reference and Research Library Agency
11 West Fortieth Street
New York, New York 10018

Subscription: Not specified
Circulation: Not specified
Frequency: Irregular

Editor: Marion L. Simmons

Indexed in: Not specified

Description: These are project reports produced for distribution to METRO members.

Contributors: METRO members. Manuscripts from other sources are neither solicited nor accepted.

Style requirements: Not applicable

Number of manuscript
copies to submit: Not applicable

Approximate length
of manuscript: Not applicable

Abstract requirement: Not applicable

Evaluation time: Not applicable

Payment: None

OCCASIONAL PAPERS IN LIBRARIANSHIP

Libraries Board of South Australia
Box 386A, G.P.O.
Adelaide, South Australia

Subscription: Varies
Circulation: Not specified
Frequency: Irregular

Editor: R. K. Olding

Address: State Library of South Australia
Box 386A, G.P.O.
Adelaide, South Australia

Indexed in: Pinpointer, Index to Australian Book Reviews

Description: This paperback series publishes facsimile or original material
on subjects relating to librarianship.

Contributors: No set policy

Style requirement: Manuscripts should be typed; no other specifications

Number of manuscript
copies to submit: One

Approximate length
of manuscript: No set policy

Abstract requirement: None

Evaluation time: Two months

Payment: None

PITTSBURGH STUDIES IN LIBRARY AND INFORMATION SCIENCES

Graduate School of Library and Information Sciences
University of Pittsburgh
Pittsburgh, Pennsylvania 15213

Subscription: Usually $3.00
Circulation: 1,000
Frequency: Irregular

Editor: Jay E. Daily

Indexed in: Not specified

Description: Research reports and studies "that are too long for periodical articles and too short for a book are reviewed for content and advancement of librarianship."

Contributors: No set policy

Style requirements: Not specified

Number of manuscript
copies to submit: One

Approximate length
of manuscript: 3,000 to 10,000 words

Abstract requirement: Required

Evaluation time: 90 days

Payment: Royalties (10%), with an advance of $100

Additional
information: Abstract and letter of inquiry should be sent before the manuscript is submitted.

PROBLEM-CENTERED APPROACHES TO LIBRARIANSHIP SERIES

R. R. Bowker Company
1180 Avenue of the Americas
New York, New York 10036

Subscription: $9.95 per volume
Circulation: Not specified
Frequency: Irregular

Editor: Thomas J. Galvin

Address: School of Library Science
Simmons College
300 The Fenway
Boston, Massachusetts 02115

Indexed in: Library Literature

Description: This new monographic series is designed to make case
studies available for instructional use in all major areas of
the library school curriculum, as well as to demonstrate
the value of the case study as a vehicle for presentation
and analysis of library problems.

Contributors: Primarily librarians

Style requirements: Information available from series editor

Number of manuscript
copies to submit: Two

Approximate length
of manuscript: Minimum of 350 manuscript pages

Abstract requirement: None

Evaluation time: 30 days

Payment: Royalties

Additional
information: Outline and text sample should be submitted in
advance to series editor.

RESEARCH STUDIES IN LIBRARY SCIENCE

Libraries Unlimited, Inc.
P.O. Box 263
Littleton, Colorado 80120

Subscription: Varies; 10% discount on standing orders
Circulation: Not specified
Frequency: Three to seven titles per year

Editor: Bohdan S. Wynar

Indexed in: Library Literature, Library and Information Science Abstracts

Description: The purpose of this series, initiated in 1970, is to provide improved access to important research studies, original research reports, significant surveys, etc. Selection of manuscripts is based on recommendations made by faculty and prominent practicing librarians.

Contributors: Primarily librarians

Style requirements: *A Manual of Style* (University of Chicago Press)

Number of manuscript
copies to submit: One

Approximate length
of manuscript: 100 to 250 pages

Abstract requirement: None

Evaluation time: Four to six weeks

Payment: Royalties

SOUTH CENTRAL RESEARCH LIBRARY COUNCIL
PAMPHLET SERIES

South Central Research Library Council
331 Sheldon Court—College Avenue
Ithaca, New York 14850

Subscription: Free to Council members
Circulation: 200
Frequency: Once or twice a year

Editor: Sylvia G. Faibisoff

Indexed in: Not specified

Description: An extension of Council publications. (The Council consists
              of 14 counties in South Central New York.)

Contributors: Only Council members

Style requirements: Not specified

Number of manuscript
copies to submit: One

Approximate length
of manuscript: 8 to 20 pages

Abstract requirement: None

Evaluation time: Not specified

Payment: None

TEXAS A AND M UNIVERSITY LIBRARY MISCELLANEOUS PUBLICATIONS

Texas A and M University Library
College Station, Texas 77843

Subscription: Varies
Circulation: Not specified
Frequency: Irregular

Editor: John B. Smith

Indexed in: Not specified

Description: Variable format. Articles are by invitation.

Contributors: Depends on the format and subject of a given issue.

Style requirements: *MLA Style Sheet*

Number of manuscript
copies to submit: Not specified

Approximate length
of manuscript: No set policy

Abstract requirement: None

Evaluation time: Not applicable

Payment: None

UNIVERSITY OF CHICAGO. STUDIES IN LIBRARY SCIENCE

University of Chicago Press
5800 Ellis
Chicago, Illinois 60637

Subscription: Varies
Circulation: Not specified
Frequency: Irregular

Editor: Editor, University of Chicago Press

Indexed in: Library Literature

Description: Monographs devoted to research in librarianship

Contributors: Librarians and faculty

Style requirements: *A Manual of Style* (University of Chicago Press)

Number of manuscript
copies to submit: One

Approximate length
of manuscript: 60,000 to 100,000 words

Abstract requirement: None

Evaluation time: Two months

Payment: Royalties

Additional
information: Most items published in the series are products of the University of Chicago Graduate Library School.

UNIVERSITY OF DENVER. STUDIES IN LIBRARIANSHIP.

Graduate School of Librarianship
University of Denver
Denver, Colorado 80210

Subscription: Varies
Circulation: Not specified
Frequency: Irregular

Editor: Faculty members at University of Denver Graduate School
of Librarianship

Indexed in: Library Literature

Description: Topics vary greatly; in general, however, they deal with
libraries, history of printing, private presses, etc.

Contributors: Students and faculty

Style requirements: Not specified

Number of manuscript
copies to submit: One

Approximate length
of manuscript: No set policy

Abstract requirement: None

Evaluation time: No set policy

Payment: None

Additional
information: There is no policy statement as such for the
occasional papers. However, the series focuses on
student and faculty studies in librarianship at the
University of Denver.

UNIVERSITY OF ILLINOIS. GRADUATE SCHOOL OF LIBRARY SCIENCE. ALLERTON PARK INSTITUTE. PAPERS.

University of Illinois
Graduate School of Library Science
Publications Office
215 Armory Building
Champaign, Illinois 61820

Subscription: Varies
Circulation: Not specified
Frequency: Annual

Editor: Varies with each issue; faculty members at University of Illinois Graduate School of Library Science

Indexed in: Not specified

Description: Proceedings of Allerton Park Institute—conferences on various aspects of librarianship.

Contributors: Speakers at the conferences.

Style requirements: Sent upon request

Number of manuscript
copies to submit: Not specified

Approximate length
of manuscript: 15 to 25 pages

Abstract requirement: None

Evaluation time: Not specified

Payment: None

Additional
information: Standing orders can be established by writing: Illini Union Bookstore, 715 South Wright, Champaign, Illinois 61820

UNIVERSITY OF ILLINOIS. GRADUATE SCHOOL OF LIBRARY SCIENCE. MONOGRAPHS.

University of Illinois
Graduate School of Library Science
Publications Office
215 Armory Building
Champaign, Illinois 61820

Subscription: Varies
Circulation: Not specified
Frequency: Irregular

Editor: Varies

Indexed in: Not specified

Description: The series includes original works dealing with some aspect of libraries and librarianship.

Contributors: Primarily librarians

Style requirements: Sent on request

Number of manuscript
copies to submit: One

Approximate length
of manuscript: 100 to 200 pages

Abstract requirement: None

Evaluation time: Two months

Payment: None

Additional
information: Standing orders can be established by writing:
Illini Union Bookstore, 715 South Wright,
Champaign, Illinois 61820

UNIVERSITY OF ILLINOIS. GRADUATE SCHOOL OF LIBRARY SCIENCE. OCCASIONAL PAPERS.

Graduate School of Library Science
University of Illinois at Urbana-Champaign
Publications Office
215 Armory Building
Champaign, Illinois 61820

Subscription: $2.00 or $3.00, depending on number of issues per year
Circulation: 1,500
Frequency: Irregular (never more than monthly)

Editor: Herbert Goldhor

Indexed in: Library Literature, Library and Information Science
               Abstracts

Description: Papers in the series cover librarianship, information science,
               or bibliography. They consist of manuscripts which because
               of length or detail generally would not be published in a
               library periodical.

Contributors: Primarily librarians

Style requirements: *A Manual of Style* (University of Chicago Press)

Number of manuscript
copies to submit: Two

Approximate length
of manuscript: 15 to 25 pages

Abstract requirement: None

Evaluation time: Four to six weeks

Payment: 12 free copies of the paper

Additional
information: Short biography should be included with the
                       manuscript.

UNIVERSITY OF ILLINOIS. GRADUATE SCHOOL OF LIBRARY SCIENCE. PROCEEDINGS OF CLINICS ON LIBRARY APPLICATIONS OF DATA PROCESSING.

Graduate School of Library Science
University of Illinois
Publications Office
215 Armory Building
Champaign, Illinois 61820

Subscription: Varies
Circulation: Not specified
Frequency: Annual

Editor: Varies; usually faculty member of the Graduate School of Library Science, University of Illinois

Indexed in: Not specified

Description: Proceedings of clinics concerning library applications of data processing.

Contributors: Speakers at the conferences.

Style requirements: Sent on request

Number of manuscript
copies to submit: One

Approximate length
of manuscript: 15 to 20 pages

Abstract requirement: None

Evaluation time: Not specified

Payment: None

Additional
information: Standing orders can be established by writing: Illini Union Bookstore, 715 South Wright, Champaign, Illinois 61820.

UNIVERSITY OF MARYLAND. SCHOOL OF LIBRARY AND INFORMATION SERVICES. CONFERENCE PROCEEDINGS.

School of Library and Information Services
University of Maryland
College Park, Maryland 20742

Subscription: Varies
Circulation: Not specified
Frequency: Irregular

Editor: Varies

Indexed in: Not specified

Description: Includes papers presented at conferences held at the University of Maryland.

Contributors: Participants in the conferences.

Style requirements: Not specified

Number of manuscript
copies to submit: Not specified

Approximate length
of manuscript: 150 to 300 pages

Abstract requirement: None

Evaluation time: No set policy

Payment: None

UNIVERSITY OF MARYLAND. SCHOOL OF LIBRARY AND INFORMATION SERVICES. STUDENT CONTRIBUTION SERIES.

School of Library and Information Service
University of Maryland
College Park, Maryland 20742

Subscription: Varies
Circulation: Not specified
Frequency: Irregular

Editor: Varies

Indexed in: Not specified

Description: Presents the perspectives of faculty and students on the social sciences. Many contributions pertain to the teaching of bibliography.

Contributors: Students and faculty

Style requirements: Not specified

Number of manuscript
copies to submit: Not specified

Approximate length
of manuscript: 100 to 250 pages

Abstract requirement: None

Evaluation time: Not specified

Payment: None

UNIVERSITY OF OREGON. OCCASIONAL PAPERS

Library
University of Oregon
Eugene, Oregon 97403

Subscription: Varies
Circulation: Not specified
Frequency: Irregular

Editor: Wilhelmina Bevers

Indexed in: Not specified

Description: Papers in the series cover librarianship, information science, and bibliography. They consist of manuscripts which because of length or detail generally would not be published in a library periodical.

Contributors: Primarily librarians

Style requirements: Not specified

Number of manuscript
copies to submit: Not specified

Approximate length
of manuscript: Not specified

Abstract requirement: None

Evaluation time: Not specified

Payment: None

Additional
information: For the past several years, none of these papers have been produced due to a tight budget. Libraries usually receive them on an exchange basis, but in some instances there is a charge.

LIBRARY-RELATED PERIODICALS

ACADEMIC THERAPY

Editorial Office
1539 Fourth Street
San Rafael, California 94901

Subscription: $6.00
Circulation: 6,000
Frequency: Quarterly

Editor: John I. Arena

Indexed in: Current Contents, Education Index, DSH Abstracts, Language and Language Behavior Abstracts, Psychological Abstracts, Rehabilitation Literature, Perceptual-Cognitive Development

Description: An interdisciplinary journal directed at teachers, parents and educational therapists worldwide. Articles on adolescents who are intellectually capable but academically under-achieving. These articles are practical rather than theoretical.

Contributors: Authorities in the field

Style requirements: *A Manual of Style* (University of Chicago Press)

Number of manuscript
copies to submit: Two

Approximate length
of manuscript: Up to 1,500 words

Abstract requirement: None

Evaluation time: Three to four weeks

Payment: None

Additional
information: No new material is being accepted until after summer, 1973.

AMERICAN BEHAVIORAL SCIENTIST

Sage Publications, Inc.
275 South Beverly Drive
Beverly Hills, California 90212

Subscription: $18.00, institutions; $12.00, educators; $9.00, students
Circulation: 2,800
Frequency: Bimonthly

Editor: Connie Greaser

Indexed in: PAIS, Mental Health Book Review Index, Sociological
               Abstracts, Psychological Abstracts, Poverty and Human
               Resources Abstracts, Social Sciences and Humanities Index

Description: Each issue is under the directorship of a special issue editor,
               who collects manuscripts suitable to a specific theme in the
               social sciences.

Contributors: Social scientists

Style requirements: Journal's style manual will be sent on request.

Number of manuscript
copies to submit: Two

Approximate length
of manuscript: 10 to 30 pages

Abstract requirement: None

Evaluation time: Four to six weeks

Payment: None

Additional
information: Unsolicited manuscripts are not accepted.

AMERICAN EDUCATIONAL RESEARCH JOURNAL (AERJ)

1126 Sixteenth Street, N.W.
Washington, D.C. 20036

Subscription: $10.00
Circulation: 11,000
Frequency: Quarterly

Editor: Kaoru Yamamoto

Address: American Educational Research Journal
College of Education
Arizona State University
Tempe, Arizona 85281

Indexed in: Education Index, Current Index to Journals in Education

Description: Experimental and theoretical papers on original research in education.

Contributors: Primarily educators

Style requirements: "Manual of Style" (1967 revision) of the American Psychological Association. Also, "Suggestions to Contributors" are on the inside front cover.

Number of manuscript
copies to submit: Three

Approximate length
of manuscript: No set policy

Abstract requirement: Required; 100 to 120 words

Evaluation time: Six to ten weeks

Payment: 50 free reprints of the article

Additional
information: Author should submit a biographical resume giving his position, office address, degrees and institutions, areas of specialization, and AERA divisional membership.

AMERICAN QUARTERLY

Box 1, Logan Hall
University of Pennsylvania
Philadelphia, Pennsylvania 19174

Subscription: $10.00; free to members of the American Studies Assn.
Circulation: 4,000
Frequency: Five times per year

Editor: Murray G. Murphey

Indexed in: Social Sciences and Humanities Index

Description: American culture, past and present, and its relationship to
               world society. Primarily bibliographies. Published by the
               University of Pennsylvania in cooperation with the American
               Studies Association.

Contributors: Scholars and librarians

Style requirements: *MLA Style Sheet*

Number of manuscript
copies to submit: Two

Approximate length
of manuscript: No set policy

Abstract requirement: Required only for literary articles (200 words)

Evaluation time: Up to five months

Payment: None

AMERICAN TEACHER

American Federation of Teachers
1012 14th Street, N.W.
Washington, D.C. 20005

Subscription: $5.00 (includes subscription to *Changing Education*)
Circulation: 250,000
Frequency: Monthly except July and August

Editor: David Elsila

Indexed in: Not specified

Description: This is the journal of the American Federation of Teachers.
               Articles relate to union activities and accomplishments such
               as legislation concerning teachers and schools, and educational
               innovations.

Contributors: Not primarily librarians

Style requirements: Not specified

Number of manuscript
copies to submit: One

Approximate length
of manuscripts: No set policy

Abstract requirement: None

Evaluation time: Up to two months

Payment: Yes

Additional
information: Query preferred prior to submission of the manu-
                       script. The American Federation of Teachers also
                       produces *Changing Education*, similar to the *Ameri-
                       can Teacher* but issued on a quarterly basis.

BEHAVIORAL SCIENCE

Mental Health Research Institute
University of Michigan
Ann Arbor, Michigan 48104

Subscription: $15.00, individuals; $30.00, institutions
Circulation: 5,000
Frequency: Bimonthly

Editor: Dr. James G. Miller

Indexed in: Sociological Abstracts, Biological Abstracts, Index Medicus, Psychological Abstracts, Mathematical Reviews

Description: Particularly interested in articles with an interdisciplinary approach, especially those dealing with the mental health field. Articles are more theoretical than practical.

Contributors: Primarily faculty members in the behavioral sciences

Style requirements: Printed on inside back cover of the journal

Number of manuscript
copies to submit: Two

Approximate length
of manuscript: Up to 3,000 words

Abstract requirement: Required (250 words or less)

Evaluation time: Two to three months

Payment: None

Additional
information: Authors are given the option of publication ahead of schedule for a charge per printed page (this charge includes 100 free reprints of the article). If the article is reprinted in another publication, the author receives half of the royalties.

CHANGE: The Magazine of Higher Learning

NBW Tower
New Rochelle, New York 10801

Subscription: $15.00; $12.00 for professionals
Circulation: 15,000
Frequency: Monthly

Editor: George W. Bonham

Indexed in: Not specified

Description: A general periodical in higher education

Contributors: Primarily educators and teachers

Style requirements: Journalistic; similar to *Atlantic Monthly*

Number of manuscript
copies to submit: One

Approximate length
of manuscript: No set policy

Abstract requirement: None

Evaluation time: Four weeks

Payment: $100 to $500

Additional
information: Over 2,000 manuscripts are received each year, but
                         unsolicited manuscripts are used only rarely.

CHANGING EDUCATION

American Federation of Teachers
1012 Fourteenth Street N.W.
Washington, D.C. 20005

Subscription: $5.00 (includes subscription to *American Teacher*)
Circulation: 250,000
Frequency: Quarterly

Editor: David Elsila

Indexed in: Education Index, Current Index to Journals in Education

Description: Carries articles dealing with developments in education (past, present, and future) and with such topics as the teacher union movement, better schools, and better educational methods.

Contributors: Primarily teachers

Style requirements: Not specified

Number of manuscript
copies to submit: One

Approximate length
of manuscripts: 750 to 2,000 words

Abstract requirement: None

Evaluation time: Three to four months

Payment: Yes

Additional
information: Photographs may be submitted with manuscripts.

COMPARATIVE EDUCATION REVIEW

208 Education Building
School of Education
University of Wisconsin
Madison, Wisconsin 53706

Subscription: $10.00
Circulation: 4,500
Frequency: Three times per year

Editor: Andreas M. Kazamias

Indexed in: Education Index

Description: Official publication of the Comparative and International
Education Society, whose purpose is to advance knowledge
and teaching in education. Comparative and analytical
articles on education in any country of the world.

Contributors: Primarily teachers and scholars familiar with comparative
education.

Style requirements: *A Manual of Style* (University of Chicago Press);
also, style information is printed on the inside
back cover of the journal.

Number of manuscript
copies to submit: Two

Approximate length
of manuscript: 4,500 to 6,000 words

Abstract requirement: Required (up to 150 words)

Evaluation time: Three to five months

Payment: None

Additional
information: Author's name and affiliation should be on a
separate page at the end of the manuscript.

DATAMATION

Technical Publishing Company
94 South Los Robles Avenue
Pasadena, California 91101

Subscription: $18.00; free to qualified personnel using automatic
information handling equipment
Circulation: 105,000
Frequency: Monthly

Editor: Robert B. Forest

Indexed in: Computer Review, Data Processing Digest

Description: Articles cover all phases of computers so that manufacturers
of electronic data processing equipment, librarians, and others
interested in datamation can be aware of recent developments
and applications of computers to information processing.

Contributors: Specialists in the field

Style requirements: "A Guide for Authors" will be sent on request.

Number of manuscript
copies to submit: One

Approximate length
of manuscript: No set policy

Abstract requirement: None

Evaluation time: Up to eight weeks

Payment: Yes

Additional
information: Outlines can be submitted for evaluation.

EDUCATION AND URBAN SOCIETY

Sage Publications, Inc.
275 South Beverly Drive
Beverly Hills, California 90212

Subscription: $15.00, institutions and educators; $8.00, students
Circulation: 1,000
Frequency: Quarterly

Editor: Jay D. Scribner

Indexed in: Poverty and Human Resources Abstracts, America: History
and Life, Historical Abstracts, Sociological Abstracts,
Sociology of Education Abstracts, Educational Abstracts,
PAIS

Description: Articles reflect research on education as an institution
affecting social change. Topics covered include the problems
and needs resulting from the national concern with improving
the urban environment, and the role of education in an
urban society.

Contributors: Social scientists

Style requirements: The journal's style sheet will be sent on request.

Number of manuscript
copies to submit: Three

Approximate length
of manuscript: 25 to 30 pages

Abstract requirement: None

Evaluation time: Four to six weeks

Payment: None

EDUCATIONAL THEORY: A Medium of Expression for the John Dewey Society and the Philosophy of Education Society

Editorial Office
Education Building
University of Illinois
Urbana, Illinois 61801

Subscription: $5.00; $8.00 for libraries and non-members
Circulation: 2,000
Frequency: Quarterly

Editor: Joe R. Burnett

Indexed in: Current Contents, Education Index, Philosopher's Index

Description: Carries articles that deal with educational theory and with other theoretical issues of concern to the education profession.

Contributors: Social scientists (especially educators)

Style requirements: Not specified

Number of manuscript
copies to submit: Four

Approximate length
of manuscript: No set policy

Abstract requirement: None

Evaluation time: Two to four months

Payment: None

HARVARD EDUCATIONAL REVIEW

Editorial and Business Office
Longfellow Hall
13 Appian Way
Cambridge, Massachusetts 02138

Subscription: $10.00; single issue, $3.00
Circulation: 12,500
Frequency: Quarterly

Editor: Kathleen Gallagher (Advertising and Manuscript Editor)

Indexed in: Education Index, PAIS, Book Review Index, Current Index
               to Journals in Education, Psychological Abstracts, Sociological
               Abstracts, Historical Abstracts, Sociology of Education
               Abstracts

Description: Articles deal with research, theory, and practice in education.

Contributors: Teachers, scholars, researchers in education, and persons in
               related fields.

Style requirements: Not specified

Number of manuscript
copies to submit: Two or more

Approximate length
of manuscripts: No set policy

Abstract requirement: Required (one page)

Evaluation time: Four to six weeks

Payment: None

Additional
information: "Articles are selected, edited, and published by an
                       Editorial Board of graduate students in Harvard
                       University." Each issue has "issue editors."

HUMAN FACTORS: The Journal of the Human Factors Society
Published by the Johns Hopkins University Press

Human Factors Society
Box 1369
Santa Monica, California 90406

Subscription: $20.00; free to members of the Society
Circulation: 2,700
Frequency: Bimonthly

Editor: Harry L. Snyder

Indexed in: Psychological Abstracts, Ergonomics Abstracts, and
Occupational Safety and Health Abstracts

Description: Articles are interdisciplinary in nature and apply to machine
and environmental factors in all their ramifications, pure
and applied. The journal carries evaluative reviews of the
literature, definitive articles on methodology and procedure,
quantitative and qualitative approaches to theory, technical
articles on original research, specific and unusual case his-
tories, utilization of information.

Contributors: Educators and scholars, and other interested individuals

Style requirements: The journal's "Manual of Style" will be sent on
request; additional information is printed on the
inside back cover of the periodical.

Number of manuscript
copies to submit: One

Approximate length
of manuscript: Up to 3,000 words

Abstract requirement: Required

Evaluation time: 90 days

Payment: 50 free reprints

Additional
information: Biographical data must be submitted.

IMPROVING COLLEGE AND UNIVERSITY TEACHING:
International Quarterly Journal

101 Waldo Hall
Oregon State University
Corvallis, Oregon 97331

Subscription: $6.00
Circulation: 3,000
Frequency: Quarterly

Editor: Delmer M. Goode

Indexed in: Education Index

Description: Carries articles on academic teaching, including libraries.

Contributors: College and university faculty members

Style requirements: Not specified

Number of manuscript
copies to submit: One

Approximate length
of manuscript: 700 to 1,400 words

Abstract requirement: Not required, but helpful

Evaluation time: "Prompt"

Payment: Four free copies of the journal

Additional
information: Because of the backlog of articles to be published, articles are grouped into themes for issues.

JOURNAL OF EDUCATIONAL RESEARCH: Dedicated to the Study of Education

Dembar Educational Research Service (DERS)
Box 1605
Madison, Wisconsin 53701

Subscription: $10.00
Circulation: 6,000
Frequency: Monthly except for May-June and July-August

Editor: Wilson B. Thiede, Wayne Otto, Robert D. Boyd

Indexed in: Education Index, Psychological Abstracts

Description: Research articles and critiques designed to advance the scientific study of education and to improve field practice.

Contributors: Primarily educators

Style requirements: Style requirements are printed on the inside back cover of the journal.

Number of manuscript copies to submit: One

Approximate length of manuscript: 1,500 to 3,000 words

Abstract requirement: Required

Evaluation time: Up to six weeks

Payment: None

Additional information: Articles are well documented and often contain illustrations.

THE JOURNAL OF EXPERIMENTAL EDUCATION

Dembar Educational Research Services (DERS)
Box 1605
Madison, Wisconsin 53701

Subscription: $10.00
Circulation: 2,000
Frequency: Quarterly

Editor: John Schmid

Address: Department of Research and Statistical Methodology
University of Northern Colorado
Greeley, Colorado 80631

Indexed in: College Student Personnel Abstracts, Current Contents,
Educational Abstracts, Education Index, Current Index to
Journals in Education, Language and Language Behavior
Abstracts

Description: Specialized or technical education studies, studies on mathe-
matics or methodology of behavioral research, and monographs of research.

Contributors: Primarily educators

Style requirements: *A Manual on Writing Research* (1962) and *A Manual
of Form for Theses and Term Reports* (1962), by
Kathleen Dugdale

Number of manuscript
copies to submit: Two

Approximate length
of manuscript: No set policy

Abstract requirement: Required (up to 120 words)

Evaluation time: Up to eight weeks

Payment: The publisher charges a contributor's fee of $6.00
per printed page of 1,200 words; the contributor
receives 10 free copies of the journal.

Additional
information: Back cover of the periodical provides additional
information on the text and style.

JOURNAL OF HIGHER EDUCATION

Ohio State University Press
2070 Neil Avenue
Columbus, Ohio 43210

Subscription: $8.00; $10.00 for libraries and organizations
Circulation: 5,500
Frequency: Monthly, October through June

Editor: Robert J. Silverman

Indexed in: Education Index, Current Index to Journals in Education,
               Bibliographic Index, Book Review Index, Abstracts for
               Social Workers, America: History and Life, Chemical
               Abstracts, Education Abstracts, Historical Abstracts, Language
               and Language Behavior Abstracts, Psychological Abstracts,
               Sociology of Education Abstracts

Description: Published by the American Association for Higher Education
               and the Ohio State University Press. Articles discuss the
               theoretical and practical issues and concepts of higher educa-
               tion; implications of research projects are also analyzed.

Contributors: Primarily educators

Style requirements: *A Manual of Style* (University of Chicago Press);
                       footnotes should be avoided.

Number of manuscript
copies to submit: Three

Approximate length
of manuscript: Three to fifteen pages

Abstract requirement: None

Evaluation time: Three to four weeks

Payment: None

MEDIA AND METHODS: Exploration in Education

North American Publishing Company
134 North Thirteenth Street
Philadelphia, Pennsylvania 19107

Subscription: $7.00
Circulation: 45,000; approximately one-half of this is controlled
Frequency: Monthly, September through May

Editor: Frank McLaughlin

Indexed in: Education Index

Description: Both solicited and unsolicited manuscripts are used. Articles deal with the audiovisual field in schools and generally attack established views about education. Most of these articles are not idealistic treatises but practical advice or guides on new approaches, techniques, and models to learning.

Contributors: Primarily teachers

Style requirements: Not specified

Number of manuscript
copies to submit: One

Approximate length
of manuscripts: Not specified

Abstract requirement: None

Evaluation time: Not specified

Payment: Not specified

Additional
information: Manuscripts will not be returned unless they are accompanied by a properly addressed envelope bearing the necessary postage.

REVIEW OF EDUCATIONAL RESEARCH

1126 Sixteenth Street, N.W.
Washington, D.C. 20036

Subscription: $10.00
Circulation: 12,500
Frequency: Five times per year

Editor: Samuel J. Messick

Address: Educational Testing Service
               Box 2604
               Princeton, New Jersey 08540

Indexed in: Education Index, Psychological Abstracts

Description: Critical reviews of research on education, interpretation, and
               analysis of substantive and methodological issues.

Contributors: Primarily educators and psychologists

Style requirements: "Publication Manual" of the American Psychological
                       Association

Number of manuscript
copies to submit: Three

Approximate length
of manuscript: No set policy

Abstract requirement: None

Evaluation time: No set policy

Payment: None

SCHOLARLY PUBLISHING: A Journal for Authors and Publishers

University of Toronto Press
Toronto 181, Canada

Subscription: $10.00
Circulation: 1,350
Frequency: Quarterly

Editor: Eleanor Harman

Indexed in: Current Contents

Description: Articles cover all phases of non-fiction publication from the inception of the book to its use by readers. Topics include editing, sales and promotion, design and production.

Contributors: Not primarily librarians

Style requirements: The journal's brochure will be sent on request.

Number of manuscript
copies to submit: One

Approximate length
of manuscript: Up to 2,000 words

Abstract requirement: None

Evaluation time: Up to one month

Payment: Yes

SCHOOL AND SOCIETY

1860 Broadway
New York, New York 10023

Subscription: $12.00
Circulation: 8,500
Frequency: Monthly, October through May

Editor: Dr. William W. Brickman

Address: Graduate School of Education
University of Pennsylvania
Philadelphia, Pennsylvania 19104

Indexed in: Education Index, Readers' Guide to Periodical Literature,
Psychological Abstracts

Description: Articles concern all aspects of college and university
activities; secondary education is also covered.

Contributors: Primarily teachers and educators

Style requirements: Style sheet will be sent on request.

Number of manuscript
copies to submit: One

Approximate length
of manuscript: 1,500 to 2,500 words

Abstract requirement: None

Evaluation time: One month

Payment: None

Additional
information: Most articles published are free-lance, although
occasionally articles are commissioned.

SOCIAL RESEARCH: An International Quarterly of the Social Sciences

New School for Social Research
66 West Twelfth Street
New York, New York 10011

Subscription: $12.00
Circulation: Not specified
Frequency: Quarterly

Editor: Dr. Arien Mack

Indexed in: PAIS, Social Sciences and Humanities Index

Description: International and interdisciplinary journal of the social
               sciences.

Contributors: Social scientists

Style requirements: Not specified

Number of manuscript
copies to submit: Two

Approximate length
of manuscript: 20 pages

Abstract requirement: None

Evaluation time: Up to two months

Payment: None

SOCIAL SCIENCE QUARTERLY
(formerly *Southwestern Social Science Quarterly*)

University of Texas at Austin
Austin, Texas 78712

Subscription: $11.00, libraries; $8.00, individuals; $5.00, students
Circulation: 3,000
Frequency: Quarterly

Editor: Charles M. Bonjean

Indexed in: PAIS, Historical Abstracts, America: History and Life, Index
              to Legal Periodicals, Sociological Abstracts, Current Contents

Description: Carries articles that deal with the social sciences and their
              interdisciplinary nature. Occasionally the journal will
              advertise that articles on specific topics are needed.

Contributors: Primarily social scientists

Style requirements: Style sheet will be sent on request.

Number of manuscript
copies to submit: Three

Approximate length
of manuscript: Up to 30 pages

Abstract requirement: Required if the article is accepted for publication.

Evaluation time: One to two months

Payment: None

SOCIOLOGICAL QUARTERLY: Journal of the Midwest
Sociological Society (formerly *Midwest Sociologist*)

1004 Elm Street
Columbia, Missouri 65201

Subscription: $7.00
Circulation: 2,200
Frequency: Quarterly

Editor: James L. McCartney

Address: University of Missouri in Columbia
               Columbia, Missouri 65201

Indexed in: Social Sciences and Humanities Index, Sociological Abstracts,
               Psychological Abstracts, Abstracts for Social Workers

Description: This is the official bulletin of the Midwest Sociological
               Society. Articles pertain to the problems and issues of
               sociology.

Contributors: Primarily sociologists

Style requirements: The style guide of the American Sociological
                       Association; also, *A Manual of Style* (University
                       of Chicago Press)

Number of manuscript
copies to submit: Three

Approximate length
of manuscript: 10 to 25 pages

Abstract requirement: Required

Evaluation time: One to three months

Payment: None

Additional
information: A comprehensive index is being prepared for the
                       journal.

SOCIOLOGY OF EDUCATION
(formerly *Journal of Educational Sociology*)

49 Sheridan Avenue
Albany, New York

Subscription: $14.00, institutions; $10.00, non-members
Circulation: 2,400
Frequency: Quarterly

Editor: Charles E. Bidwell

Address: Department of Sociology
Northwestern University
Evanston, Illinois 60201

Indexed in: Education Index, Psychological Abstracts, Current Index
to Journals in Education

Description: Articles analyze educational institutions on an international
basis, stressing interdisciplinary studies.

Contributors: Social scientists

Style requirements: Printed on verso of title page of the journal

Number of manuscript
copies to submit: Two

Approximate length
of manuscript: No set policy

Abstract requirement: Required

Evaluation time: Eight weeks to five months

Payment: None

THE TEACHER PAPER

2221 N.E. 23rd Street
Portland, Oregon 97212

Subscription: $2.00
Circulation: 2,500
Frequency: Quarterly

Editor: Fred L. Staab

Indexed in: Not specified

Description: This quarterly is designed for parents, teachers, and administrators of public schools, with the aim of "rocking the boat" of public schools. Presents anecdotes from the classroom and teacher problems, successes and failures.

Contributors: Classroom teachers, pre-school through twelfth grade

Style requirements: Not specified

Number of manuscript
copies to submit: One

Approximate length
of manuscript: 500 to 2,000 words

Abstract requirement: None

Evaluation time: One month

Payment: One cent per word

Additional
information: Short biographical data should be included. Editorial deadlines are September 1, November 1, January 1, and March 1.

TODAY'S EDUCATION
(formerly *NEA Journal*)

National Education Association
1201 Sixteenth Street, N.W.
Washington, D.C. 20036

Subscription: $1.05; free to members; single issue, $0.80
Circulation: 1,250,000
Frequency: Monthly, September to May

Editor: Mildred S. Fenner

Indexed in: Readers' Guide to Periodical Literature, Education Index, Psychological Abstracts

Description: Carries articles on teaching methods and practices, and human interest stories from nursery school to adult education.

Contributors: Primarily teachers

Style requirements: "Suggestions for Authors" will be sent on request.

Number of manuscript
copies to submit: One

Approximate length
of manuscript: 800 to 2,500 words

Abstract requirement: None

Evaluation time: Two weeks to three months

Payment: None for articles; for photographs of school situations and scenes, $10.00 to $100.00.

URBAN EDUCATION

Sage Publications
275 South Beverly Drive
Beverly Hills, California 90212

Subscription: $15.00, institutions; $10.00, individuals; $7.50, students
Circulation: 1,000
Frequency: Quarterly

Editor: Warren Button

Address: Department of Social Foundation of Education
               State University of New York at Buffalo
               305 Foster Hall
               Buffalo, New York 14214

Indexed in: Biological Abstracts, Sociology of Education Abstracts,
               Poverty and Human Resources Abstracts, Educational
               Abstracts, Current Index to Journals in Education

Description: Articles are designed to improve the quality of urban
               education by publicizing the results of relevant empirical
               studies.

Contributors: Educators and specialists from other relevant fields

Style requirements: "Notes to Contributors" will be sent on request.

Number of manuscript
copies to submit: Two

Approximate length
of manuscript: Up to 25 pages

Abstract requirement: None

Evaluation time: Four to six weeks

Payment: None

Additional
information: This journal can generally use review essays,
                      bibliographic articles, and bibliographic compila-
                      tions. Contributors should send an inquiry to the
                      editor before submitting a manuscript.

APPENDIX I

ADDITIONAL MONOGRAPHIC SERIES

ACRL Monograph Series
Association of College and Research Libraries
American Library Association
50 East Huron Street
Chicago, Illinois 60611

   The American Library Association has many series pertaining to library science, such as the Library Technology Program Publications series and the Small Libraries Project series. These and others are listed in the ALA catalog of publications.

Case Studies in Library Science
Shoe String Press, Inc.
995 Sherman Avenue
Hamden, Connecticut 06514

   Shoe String Press also distributes books under the imprints of Linnet Books and Archon Books, published by Clive Bingley in London.

Contributions to Library Literature
Shoe String Press, Inc.
995 Sherman Avenue
Hamden, Connecticut 06514

Examination Guide Series
Shoe String Press, Inc.
995 Sherman Avenue
Hamden, Connecticut 06514

Frontiers of Librarianship
School of Library Science
Syracuse University
Syracuse, New York 13210

Guides to Subject Literature
Shoe String Press, Inc.
995 Sherman Avenue
Hamden, Connecticut 06514

Information Sources for Research and Development
Shoe String Press, Inc.
995 Sherman Avenue
Hamden, Connecticut 06514

Latin American Historical Dictionaries Series
Scarecrow Press
52 Liberty Street
Metuchen, N.J., 08840

Scarecrow Press publishes several other series that can be identified through the Scarecrow Press catalog.

The Management of Change
Shoe String Press, Inc.
995 Sherman Avenue
Hamden, Connecticut 06514

Programmed Texts in Library and Information Science
Shoe String Press, Inc.
995 Sherman Avenue
Hamden, Connecticut 06514

Studies in Library Management
Shoe String Press, Inc.
995 Sherman Avenue
Hamden, Connecticut 06514

World Classics of Librarianship
Shoe String Press, Inc.
995 Sherman Avenue
Hamden, Connecticut 06514

APPENDIX II

OUT-OF-PRINT PUBLICATIONS

In the process of corresponding with various editors, the compilers were notified that certain series and journals were no longer in publication. Some of the occasional papers series, for example, have not been published in the past several years and there are no plans to issue any more works in the series. Thus, most of these asked not to be included in the directory. Others have ceased publication and have been superseded by other publications. In such cases the authors have tried to include the new publications when appropriate. A list of out-of-print publications follows.

Bibliographic Series
Pennsylvania State University
University Libraries
University Park, Pennsylvania 16802

Bio-Bibliographical Series
University of Colorado Libraries
Boulder, Colorado 80302

College Library Notes for the College President
Association of American Colleges
1818 R Street, N.W.
Washington, D.C. 20009

Cornell Library Journal
Olin Library
Cornell University Library
Ithaca, New York 14850

Drexel Library School Series
Graduate School of Library Science
Drexel Institute of Technology
32nd and Chestnut Streets
Philadelphia, Pennsylvania 19104

Educational Media
1015 Florence Street
Fort Worth, Texas, 76102

North County Libraries
20 Park Street
Concord, New Hampshire 03301

North Western Group. Occasional Papers
Reference, Special and Information Section
Faculty of Community Studies
Manchester Polytechnic
Aytour Street
Manchester MI 3GH, England

Ohio State University Library Notes
Ohio State University Libraries
Columbus, Ohio 43203

Progress in Library Science
Butterworth's and Company
14 Curity Avenue
Toronto 16, Ontario
Canada

Research Series
Illinois State Library
Springfield, Illinois 62706

School Series
Pennsylvania State University
University Libraries
University Park, Pennsylvania 17802

SUBJECT INDEX

Periodicals and series are entered in this index according to areas of their primary emphasis. Only those journals that are general in nature (i.e., *Library Journal* and *Wilson Library Bulletin*) are entered under all general headings. Numbers in italics refer to annuals, monographic series, and irregular publications, many of which publish manuscripts longer than journal articles.

SUBJECT INDEX

212

SUBJECT INDEX

TITLE INDEX

This index includes titles from the three sections of the directory, plus the two appendices.

TITLE INDEX

TITLE INDEX